UNIVERSITY OF NORTH CAROLINA AT CHAPEL HILL
DEPARTMENT OF ROMANCE LANGUAGES

NORTH CAROLINA STUDIES
IN THE ROMANCE LANGUAGES AND LITERATURES

ESSAYS; TEXTS, TEXTUAL STUDIES AND TRANSLATIONS; SYMPOSIA

Founder: URBAN TIGNER HOLMES

Distributed by:

UNIVERSITY OF NORTH CAROLINA PRESS
CHAPEL HILL
North Carolina 27514
U.S.A.

NORTH CAROLINA STUDIES IN THE
ROMANCE LANGUAGES AND LITERATURES

Essays
Number 4

VOLTAIRE AND THE FRENCH ACADEMY

VOLTAIRE AND THE FRENCH ACADEMY

BY
KARLIS RACEVSKIS

CHAPEL HILL

NORTH CAROLINA STUDIES IN THE ROMANCE
LANGUAGES AND LITERATURES
U.N.C. DEPARTMENT OF ROMANCE LANGUAGES
1975

Library of Congress Cataloging in Publication Data

Racevskis, Karlis.
    Voltaire and the French Academy.
    (North Carolina Studies in the Romance Languages and Literatures: Essays; 4)

    Bibliography: p. 137.
    1. Voltaire, François Marie Arouet de, 1694-1778—Friends and associates. 2. Académie française, Paris.
I. Title. II. Series: North Carolina Studies in the Romance Languages and Literatures: Essays; 4.

PQ2105.A2R3   848'.5'09   74-26585
ISBN 9780807891636

DEPÓSITO LEGAL: V. 3.759 - 1975

ARTES GRÁFICAS SOLER, S. A. - JÁVEA, 28 - VALENCIA (8) - 1975

To my parents

ACKNOWLEDGEMENTS

Since my book started out as a doctoral dissertation, I wish to express my gratitude to Professor Jean Sareil, of Columbia University, for suggesting a highly rewarding topic and for providing a sure and careful guidance through the intricacies of an extremely rich period. Likewise, I am thankful to Professor Gita May for her judicious corrections and valuable suggestions. The toils and talents of my wife Maija relieved me of the technical and mechanical side of the work; I am grateful for her help and for the moral support she provided.

I am also indebted to the Antioch College Humanities Area Faculty Development Fund Committee, whose Ford Foundation grant greatly facilitated the writing of this study. Lastly, I wish to acknowledge a grant from the Wright State University Foundation, which helped make the publication of my work possible.

TABLE OF CONTENTS

	Page
INTRODUCTION	13
CHAPTER	
I. THE LONG ROAD TO THE ACADEMY	17
II. THE "NEGLECTED" ACADEMY	51
III. THE ACADEMIC BATTLEGROUND	70
IV. THE CITADEL OF LETTERS	93
V. THE ACADEMY'S TRIBUTE	117
CONCLUSION	127
APPENDIXES	131
BIBLIOGRAPHY	137

INTRODUCTION

The life and literary career of Voltaire is a topic so vast and intricate, that even after innumerable works on the subject, relatively unexplored facets of this rich existence still remain to be studied. The history of Voltaire's relationship with the French Academy is one such area. Although many facts about this history are known and certain portions of it have already been examined, a full account of the relationship has not yet been written.

The biographies of Voltaire and the works on the French Academy that deal with this aspect of the philosophe's life have usually presented the more salient events in the relationship as separate occurrences, and have generally failed to view them in the light of the beliefs that governed Voltaire's conduct. The philosophe was doubtless mercurial in his moods and often contradictory in the opinions he expressed on various subjects. Nevertheless, there were principles to which he held steadfastly throughout his life. His involvement with the Academy spans a period of almost fifty years: it was sufficiently long and intense to make us suspect that his attachment to the Company of Immortals was more than casual.

To date, the fullest account of the relationship has been given by Lucien Brunel in *Les Philosophes et l'Académie française au dix-huitième siècle*. Unfortunately, Brunel's treatment of Voltaire suffers from two deficiencies. First, the author judges continuously on the basis of his own ethical principles. As a result, he views with contempt many of those actions which, while being characteristic of Voltaire's conduct, were also part of a very effective strategy designed to avoid persecution and to defend the cause of the philosophe party. Secondly, Brunel sees Voltaire as a man obsessed with the "cause," often unrealistic and irrational in his efforts to further the aims of the philosophes within the Academy. He ignores Voltaire, the man of letters, to whom the Company was much more than a philosophic battleground.

We have found it necessary to distinguish between two motivating principles which guided Voltaire in his relations with the Academy: his concern for the Enlightenment on the one hand, and his love of French letters on the other. There are instances when it becomes difficult to separate the two concerns, but in order to understand clearly Voltaire's attitude towards the Academy, it is necessary to determine the relative importance of these motives. To do that, we must view them separately.

A study of Voltaire's relationship with the Company of Immortals from the perspective of these general principles will also help us to explore some of the biographical clichés that have gained authority by having been repeated often enough. Such, for example, is the assertion that Voltaire lost all interest in the Academy soon after his election, and that this apparent ingratitude lasted for more than ten years. There is also the well known story of Voltaire's relations with the *président* de Brosses, according to which the Patriarch of Ferney denied a worthy candidate admission to the Academy because of a ten-year-old quarrel over some cut wood. In those instances where the present thesis will not challenge traditionally accepted versions, we hope to provide an additional dimension to the understanding of Voltaire's actions and reactions.

While the discussion of Voltaire's attitudes concerning the Academy will make up the central theme of the study, we will also have occasion to comment on the important part played by the French Academy in the political and cultural life of Eighteenth-century France. One particular aspect of this topic concerns the role that the Academy had in the struggles of the philosophe party. We shall use the term "party" rather loosely here, with the understanding that, although the philosophes did share a few general ideals, they never formed a homogeneous group; their aims and methods often differed from individual to individual. The question of using the Academy as a vehicle for the new ideas was as controversial as any other and created dissent even among those who favored this tactic. Voltaire's views on this subject were not always approved by the other philosophe members of the Academy. By comparing the various attitudes and by weighing the proportions of illusion and realism that made up the diverging beliefs of Voltaire and of his *confrères,* we will be offering a commentary on the importance of the Academy in the history of the Enlightenment. We hope to clear up, in this manner, a few misconceptions about the learned society, for which Voltaire himself has been partly responsible.

While realizing that a number of the events and situations covered by this study could lend themselves to a more thorough treatment, we have avoided very detailed digressions in order to preserve the basic purpose behind our work. We have tried to present the relationship of the writer and the Company as a story possessing a fundamental unity, and to trace as parallel developments the theme of Voltaire's attitude on the one hand, and the history of the Institution on the other. This dual approach will prove helpful, we hope, in elucidating certain chapters in both the life of Voltaire and the history of the French Academy.

Chapter I

THE LONG ROAD TO THE ACADEMY

Voltaire's struggle to be elected to the French Academy was especially long and arduous for one obvious reason: he was deemed unacceptable both by the members of the Academy and by the outside forces controlling its membership. This situation may appear at first as a puzzling contradiction, since Voltaire was already the outstanding literary figure of his country when he first sought to be elected to the Academy. In order to resolve this paradox, we must first understand what the French Academy had become by 1731, almost a hundred years after its foundation, at the time when the possibility of Voltaire's candidacy was first mentioned.

The French Academy had been founded in 1635 in accordance with the wishes of Richelieu and had developed under the great cardinal's protection. The aims of the Company were outlined in the statutes: "La principale fonction de l'Académie sera de travailler avec tout le soin et toute la diligence possibles à donner des règles certaines à notre langue et à la rendre pure, éloquente et capable de traiter les arts et les sciences." [1] In addition to these purely grammatical and linguistical influences, the Academy was to have a determining role on an aesthetic level as well. Richelieu had intended it to be a type of literary tribunal, a "supreme court of literature." The Academy was to set the example through the works and publications of its members; it could also pass judgment on the writings of others.

---

[1] *Les Registres de l'Académie française* (Paris: Didot, 1895-1906), IV, 25. To avoid unnecessary footnotes, all subsequent references to this work will appear parenthetically in the text as "Registres."

The famous opinion on Corneille's *Le Cid* (1637) was the first verdict of this nature.

Unfortunately, these commendable plans were rather short-lived. They suffered a most serious setback in 1672, when Louis XIV, the protector of all arts, decided to become the protector of a company that had acquired renown and distinction in the field of letters. Thus, in the latter part of the seventeenth century, matters concerning language and literature found themselves relegated to a secondary rank of importance and the principal concern of the Academy became the writing and reciting of panegyrics directed at its august protector. The statement made by the Archbishop of Noyon in 1699 gives this tradition the weight of an unwritten statute: "Le principal objet de l'Académie est de consacrer le nom de l'incomparable Louis à l'immortalité." [2]

It is worth pointing out, however, that the Company's prestige did not suffer exceedingly from this situation. The Academy could still be regarded as the high court of French letters, because its membership included the most illustrious literary figures of the time. Racine, La Fontaine, Boileau, Thomas Corneille, Chapelle, Fontenelle, Fénelon, La Bruyère, La Motte, and Dacier were all elected to the Academy during the protectorate of Louis XIV. The notable exception was Molière, who was never admitted because he was an actor.

The list of Academicians who occupied the forty chairs in 1731, the year when Voltaire first considered entering the Citadel of the Immortals, shows us a changed Academy, lacking much of the brilliance that had formerly been associated with its status as "tribunal littéraire." [3] Half of its seats were occupied by members of the clergy (most of whom had negligible or nonexistent literary reputations), the rest by an assortment of *grands seigneurs,* military men, ministers, and a few men of letters. It is true that Academicians possessing real literary merit or genuine scholarly aptitude had always formed a minority in the Academy. Talent was, however, becoming increasingly scarce among the Immortals during the first decades of the eighteenth century and the Company was incurring growing discredit.

---

[2] Paul Mesnard, *Histoire de l'Académie française depuis sa fondation jusqu'en 1830* (Paris: Charpentier, 1857), p. 30.

[3] A list of the members of the French Academy in 1731 is given in Appendix A, pp. 131-132.

This invasion by non-literary Academicians was not carried out overnight. It can be traced back to the last decades of the seventeenth century: "Dans les dernières années du règne de Louis XIV les grands seigneurs et les prélats y étaient entrés en nombre ... quelques-unes des élections à peine se justifient par le mérite littéraire des élus, les autres ne s'expliquent que par la situation que ces académiciens occupaient à la cour." [4]

The title of Academician had become a fashionable and coveted honor and men of letters found themselves competing with very powerful candidates. Quality of birth and rank in society had become the predominant factors that could open the doors to the Academy. Outside influences played a leading role in the elections and a candidacy to a vacant chair gave rise to intrigues and *cabales* that involved various personalities of the court and of high society, even of the ministry. Lucien Brunel offers a particularly vivid account of this state of affairs:

> De platitude en platitude, l'Académie passe par tous les degrés de l'intolérance, prend un masque de dévotion, obéit à tous les caprices, non plus du roi, d'un grand roi, mais d'un ministre ombrageux, puis du précepteur, vilain petit prêtre sans esprit ni talent; écarte les écrivains qu'elle voudrait prendre et qui lui feraient honneur, accepte sans les connaître des gens qui sont à la cour ceci ou cela. C'est une servitude sans limite, sans issue; tout le monde, sauf les gens de lettres, exerce des droits sur ses suffrages: la reine, les favorites, toute la cour, toutes les grandes dames; celles-ci pour les officiers de leur maison ou pour leurs courtisans, celles-là bientôt pour leurs amants. [5]

Some of the fashionable salons of the period had become veritable brokerage houses of academic seats. The most famous was the salon of Mme de Lambert. It was the most influential and also the most successful in this respect, judging from letters written by her contemporaries. D'Argenson notes in his memoirs: "On lui avait même donné l'air ridicule d'une chose réelle, qui est qu'on n'était guère

---

[4] Emile Gassier, *Les Cinq cents Immortels: Histoire de l'Académie française, 1634-1906* (Paris: Jouve, 1906), p. 89.

[5] Lucien Brunel, *Les Philosophes et l'Académie française au dix-huitième siècle* (Paris: Hachette, 1884), p. 18. The "ministre ombrageux" designates the cardinal de Fleury.

reçu à l'Académie qu'on n'allât chez elle se faire présenter, quand même on eût été peu connu. Il est certain qu'elle avait bien fait la moitié des académiciens."⁶ Similarly, the Academician Bouhier remarked in a letter written in 1727 that: "Elle a furieusement de crédit parmi nos frères."⁷ Also influential, though perhaps to a lesser degree, were later the salons of Mme de Tencin, Mme d'Aiguillon, Mme Du Deffand, and Mme Geoffrin.

The prestige of the Academy had, as a result, suffered a noticeable decline. There was a genuine concern, both inside and outside the Academy, over the rapid deterioration of the Company. Already towards the end of the seventeenth century Segrais had sensed the danger that the influx of the new candidates represented for the learned Society: "Les gens de qualité que l'on introduit dans l'Académie Française en si grand nombre lui font grand tort. Il faut qu'il y en ait; mais le nombre devrait être fixé à sept ou huit, et les autres Académiciens devraient être choisis dans toutes sortes de belles-Littératures."⁸ One of the most serious and devoted members of the Academic body, the abbé d'Olivet, echoed these sentiments some thirty years later in a letter to Bouhier, where he commented on the intrigues that led to the election of Séguy in 1735. He deplored the state of the Academy and warned: "Il est à propos qu'elle pense sérieusement à elle, car vous ne sauriez croire combien elle perd depuis quelques années.... Je voudrais que la docte compagnie fît ses choix avec plus de circonspection."⁹ As writer of the Academy's official history (which was a continuation of the work started by Pellisson) d'Olivet was in a particularly good position to evaluate the organization. In an earlier letter to *président* Rose, dated 27 August 1733, he had explained his reasons for not continuing his history past the year 1700: "A mesure que nous avançons, le nombre des seigneurs et des prélats ne fait que croître dans notre Académie. Or, il n'y a pas de plaisir à parler

---

⁶ René-Louis de Voyer, marquis d'Argenson, *Journal et Mémoires du Marquis d'Argenson*, ed. J. B. Rathery (Paris: Renouard, 1859), I, 164.

⁷ Emmanuel de Broglie, *Les Portefeuilles du Président Bouhier* (Paris: Hachette, 1896), p. 176.

⁸ Jean Renaud de Segrais, *Œuvres diverses* (Amsterdam: Changuion, 1732), I, 14.

⁹ P. Pellisson-Fontanier and Pierre-Joseph Thoulier d'Olivet, *Histoire de l'Académie française par Pellisson et d'Olivet* (Paris: Livet, 1858), II, 429 and 431.

d'eux ... le bon sens demande qu'on s'attache principalement à ce qu'il y a de littéraire." [10]

A prevalent attitude adopted by persons outside the Academy was that of open mockery. Elections were often greeted with sarcasms; candidacies were commented upon and ridiculed. In 1721, Montesquieu had Rica of the *Lettres Persanes* make the following observations:

> J'ai ouï parlé d'une espèce de tribunal qu'on appelle l'Académie française. Il n'y en a point de moins respecté dans le monde; car on dit qu'aussitôt qu'il a décidé le peuple casse ses arrêts, et lui impose des lois qu'il est obligé de suivre.... Ceux qui le composent n'ont d'autre fonction que de jaser sans cesse: l'éloge va se placer comme de lui-même dans leur babil éternel; et sitôt qu'ils sont initiés dans ses mystères, la fureur du panégyrique vient les saisir, et ne les quitte plus. Ce corps a quarante têtes toutes remplies de figures, de métaphores et d'antithèses; tant de bouches ne parlent que par exclamation.... Il n'est point ferme sur ses pieds; car le temps, qui est son fléau, l'ébranle à tous les instants, et détruit ce qu'il a fait. [11]

In 1731, the Parisian lawyer Marais, who kept Bouhier abreast of the latest developments in the Academy, informed his correspondent that "M. le comte de Gramont se présente pour remplir la place de M. de la Faye. Mme de Gontaut, Mme de Rupelmonde et d'autres dames veulent avoir un résident à l'Académie, et il en servira. Il joue bien au piquet et décidera s'il faut dire en jouant 'une levée' ou 'un lever'." [12] Doubtless, many of the critics were expressing resentment caused by the rebuff their own candidacies had experienced, but a few of the Academy's choices were outrageous enough to justify these satirical outbursts. There was, for example, the scandal caused by the election of l'abbé Séguy, mentioned earlier, who became an Academician thanks to the intimate relationship he enjoyed with the maréchale de Villars. [13] A few of the seats seemed to be hereditary; the chair of Coislin had been occupied by three members of the same

---

[10] *Ibid.*, II, 385-386.

[11] Montesquieu, *Œuvres complètes* (Paris: Gallimard, 1949), I, 242-243. Having derided the Company, Montesquieu nevertheless sought its favors a few years later and was elected in 1727.

[12] de Broglie, p. 195.

[13] Pellisson and d'Olivet, II, 428-430.

family. Certain posts, such as that of the *bibliothécaire du roi* and that of *précepteur* and *sous-précepteur du Dauphin*, automatically entitled their holders to a seat in the Academy. The case of Voltaire himself, compared to that of his life-long friend, the maréchal de Richelieu, provides us with one of the best illustrations of the Academy's inequities in the selection of its members. Richelieu (who was two years younger than Voltaire) was elected to the Academy in 1720, at the age of 24 — a full 26 years before Voltaire. He was evidently incapable of writing an inaugural discourse and engaged Fontenelle, Campistron, and Destouches each to write a reception oration for him. The duke then made a composite of the three discourses using his own peculiar brand of spelling.[14]

Voltaire, of course, contributed his share to the barbs that assailed the Academy during this period of decadence. He was only eighteen when he took his first swipe at the Institution. It was on the occasion of Danchet's election to the Academy in 1712. The candidate was a minor literary figure of the time and owed his success principally to the ardent campaigning of Mme de Ferriol and her sister, Mme de Tencin.[15] Voltaire commented in verse:

> Danchet, si méprisé jadis,
> Fait voir aux pauvres de génie
> Qu'on peut gagner l'Académie
> Comme on gagne le paradis.[16]

Some twenty years later, in his famous *Lettres philosophiques,* Voltaire mocked the rhetoric that had become traditional in the Academy. The passage is well known but deserves repetition:

> Tout ce que j'entrevois dans ces beaux discours, c'est que le récipiendaire ayant assuré que son prédécesseur était un grand homme, que le cardinal de Richelieu était un très grand homme, le chancelier Seguier un assez grand homme, Louis XIV un plus que grand homme, le directeur lui répond la

---

[14] Louis-François Faur, *Vie privée du Maréchal de Richelieu* (Paris: Buisson, 1791), I, 114.
[15] Jean Sareil, *Les Tencin* (Geneva: Droz, 1969), p. 40.
[16] Voltaire, *Œuvres complètes,* ed. Louis Moland (Paris: Garnier Frères, 1877-1885), X, 470. Subsequent references to the works of Voltaire will appear parenthetically in the text as "Moland."

même chose, et ajoute que le récipiendaire pourrait bien aussi être une espèce de grand homme, et que pour lui directeur, il n'en quitte pas sa part. (Moland, XXII, 184)

In spite of his mockery, Voltaire was more than eager to win the glory that appeared so empty to some of his contemporaries. He readily acknowledged this seeming paradox in the *Lettre sur les inconvénients attachés à la littérature,* and pointed out that "cette Académie française est l'objet secret des vœux de tous les gens de lettres, c'est une maîtresse contre laquelle ils font des chansons et des épigrammes, jusqu'à ce qu'ils aient obtenu ses faveurs." [17]

In view of the convictions shared by most Academicians and considering the circumstances that governed the functioning of the Academy, Voltaire's chances of winning one of the chairs seemed slim indeed. We have seen that literary accomplishments were classed only secondary in the criteria that determined admission to the Academy. Even as a distinguished writer, Voltaire failed to qualify on two major points: he was obviously unorthodox in religious matters, and his name in general had an undesirable aura of notoriety about it. In order to better understand the difficulties that Voltaire faced as a candidate, let us review briefly the factors and events that had contributed to forming Voltaire's public image in 1731.

Although he had not yet become the well known adversary of "l'Infâme," his reputation was already considerably tainted in the eyes of the more orthodox segment of society. Voltaire had been known to espouse daring opinions for a good number of years: "Dès ses premiers pas littéraires Voltaire a été considéré comme un esprit frondeur." [18] In his *Vie de Voltaire* Condorcet tells us of Father Le Jay, who had predicted that his pupil one day "serait en France le coryphée du

---

[17] Voltaire, *Voltaire's Correspondence,* ed. Theodore Besterman (Geneva: Institut et Musée Voltaire, 1953-1965), II, 423. Subsequent references to this edition will appear parenthetically in the text as "Best." followed by the number of the letter. In the case of appendixes, volume and page numbers will be given. It is also to be noted that we have followed the practice of Besterman's edition which reproduces the original spelling of all letters available in manuscript form.

[18] Jean Sareil, "Voltaire et le Cardinal de Fleury," *Revue annuelle de la Société française d'étude du XVIIIe siècle,* No. 2 (Paris: Garnier Frères, 1970), p. 43.

déisme" (Moland, I, 191). The young Voltaire was noticed for his bold ideas outside of school as well. He was sent by his father to Caen in 1713, and while he was there, "il scandalisa les personnes pieuses, en lisant partout des poésies qui ne respiraient ni la religion ni la morale la plus édifiante." [19]

Voltaire had experienced his first conflict with the authorities in 1714 when he was sent into exile after writing "Le Bourbier." Earlier that year the young Arouet had submitted an ode to the regular competition organized by the Academy. The award, however, went to a certain abbé du Jarry. The abbé's poem contained the line "des pôles glacés aux pôles brûlants." Voltaire jeered at this unscientific blunder, disparaging the author for having written it, and the Academy for having crowned it. In his disappointment Voltaire wrote a poem attacking principally the dramatic author and poet Houdar de La Motte, who was responsible for the Academy's decision. In the poem he speaks of

> Un bourbier noir, d'infecte profondeur,
> Qui fait sentir très-malplaisante odeur
> A tout chacun, fors à la troupe impure
> Qui va nageant dans ce fleuve d'ordure.
>   (Moland, X, 77)

Among the dwellers of the bog there are the "jetonniers," [20] two of whom (Houdar de La Motte and Terrasson) are mentioned by name.

The young poet was exiled again two years later because "on lui reprochait d'avoir laissé courir des épigrammes contre le Régent et la duchesse de Berry, sa fille." [21] Then, in 1717, the Regent was offended by the publication of two anonymous satirical poems — *Puero regnante* and *J'ai vu*. Although Voltaire's authorship of the poems was never proven, he was forced to spend eleven months in the Bastille (from 17 May 1717 to 11 April 1718) as a result of their appearance. In 1726 Voltaire returned to the Bastille as a result of his quarrel with the chevalier de Rohan. On the occasion of this second incarceration,

---

[19] Léon Crouslé, *La Vie et les œuvres de Voltaire* (Paris: Honoré Champion, 1899), I, 27.

[20] Derisive term for Academicians; they were paid with a "jeton" for attending each meeting.

[21] François Ravaisson, *Archives de la Bastille* (Paris: Durand, 1866-1904), XII, 87.

René Hérault, the *Lieutenant Général* of the police in Paris, received an anonymous letter which shows us rather vividly what a certain segment of society thought of Voltaire: "Vous venez de mettre à la Bastille un homme que je souhaitais y voir il y a plus de 15 années... tout homme qui se déclare ennemi de Jésus Christ, notre divin maître et bon sauveur, est un impie que nous devons poursuivre à cor et à cris" (Best. 269, 25 April 1726).

The next publication to disturb the authorities was the poem concerning the death of Mlle Lecouvreur. It appeared in 1730, following Voltaire's return from England. The implications contained in Voltaire's comparison of France and England were not lost on the readers:

> Ah! verrai-je toujours ma faible nation,
> Incertaine en ses vœux, flétrir ce qu'elle admire;
> Nos mœurs avec nos lois toujours se contredire,
> Et le Français volage endormi sous l'empire
>   De la superstition?
> Quoi! n'est-ce donc qu'en Angleterre
> Que les mortels osent penser?
>
>   (Moland, IX, 370)

Alarmed at the furor caused by the poem and fearing exile, Voltaire spread the rumor that he had returned to England.

By this time, all of Voltaire's literary creations were regarded with suspicion. Thus, when the *Histoire de Charles XII* appeared in 1731, the first edition was immediately seized by the police. Judgments were passed on hearsay, and the book did not have to be read in order to be condemned: "La Vie du roi de Suède par Voltaire, est bien écrite à ce qu'on dit, mais bien partiale contre la France. Voilà un Français traître à sa patrie et bien fou; il est tantôt pour tantôt contre, selon que sa plume le mène, et il ne tient à rien qu'il ne renverse ciel et terre." As a result, quite serious and explicit accusations were directed at Voltaire: "C'est un anti-monarque, et il ne paraît pas respecter beaucoup les puissances de la terre." [22]

The injustice of these ready-made verdicts gave Voltaire good reason for complaint. He could not avoid drawing a parallel between himself and an author treated with much more favor:

---

[22] Mathieu Marais, *Journal et Mémoires sur la Régence et le Règne de Louis XV* (Paris: Firmin Didot Frères, 1863-1868), III, 325 and 327.

> Il y a des temps où l'on peut impunément faire les choses les plus hardies, il y en a d'autres où ce qu'il y a de plus simple et de plus innocent devient dangereux et criminel. Y a-t-il rien de plus fort que les lettres persannes? Y a-t-il un livre ou l'on ait traité le gouvernement et la relligion avec moins de ménagement? Ce livre cependant n'a produit autre chose que de faire entrer son auteur dans la trouppe nommée académie française. (Best. 615, to Cideville, 26 July 1733)

Voltaire, however, does not mention the fact that, in order to become Academician, Montesquieu denied authorship of the original version of the *Lettres persanes,* and after deleting the more daring passages, presented a new edition to the Cardinal de Fleury. Although he was not duped by this stratagem, the cardinal was satisfied with the recantation and approved Montesquieu's candidacy. Voltaire later recounted the incident in his *Siècle de Louis XIV* (Moland, XIV, 106-107).

In order to establish himself as a serious candidate for a seat in the Academy, Voltaire had, therefore, a task which presented two major difficulties. First, he had to avoid any further trouble, and second, he somehow had to clear his name. The first condition was impossible to fulfill. Even though Voltaire constantly strove to flatter the authorities, there was something in his nature that prevented him from ever becoming a good courtier. Lanson presents a lucid analysis of this seeming contradiction in Voltaire's character: "Il ne sait se défaire ni de son âme de courtisan ni de son âme de philosophe, et tandis qu'il prend des postures indécentes pour un homme qui pense, les vérités qu'il lâche, sont, chez un homme de cour, des maladresses ou des impertinences." [23] It seemed just as difficult to meet the challenge posed by the second condition. On the other hand, Voltaire's desire to become one of the Immortals was intense. It sustained his resolve during fifteen years of intermittent struggle and gave new impetus to his will following each new disappointment.

We have already stated that the possibility of Voltaire's candidacy was first mentioned in 1731. On the occasion of a vacancy produced by the death of La Faye that year, Bouhier discussed the search for new candidates in a letter to Marais, and wondered: "Le retour si prompt de Voltaire ne vous fait-il pas soupçonner qu'il a quelques

---

[23] Gustave Lanson, *Voltaire* (Paris: Hachette, 1906), p. 26.

vues de ce côté-là?" [24] Marais found no basis for this supposition: "Voltaire ne songe point à l'Académie, et l'Académie ne songe point à lui." [25]

In December Houdar de La Motte died, and Marais thought that Voltaire would be a worthy candidate, preferable to others who had already been proposed: "On lui désigne pour successeur M. de Moncrif, qui a fait les *Chats*. J'aimerais bien mieux notre Voltaire, poète, historien, orateur, critique et tout ce qu'il lui plaît d'être." [26] Condorcet notes that Voltaire explored the possibilities of becoming one of the Immortals at the time, but that he immediately met with a categorical refusal: "Il crut alors pouvoir aspirer à une place à l'Académie française, et on pouvait le trouver modeste d'avoir attendu si longtemps; mais il n'eut même pas le bonheur de balancer les suffrages. Le Gros de Boze prononça, d'un ton doctoral, que Voltaire ne serait jamais un personnage académique" (Moland, I, 203). Gros de Boze, scholar and numismatist, was one of the more influential members of the Academy. He was also an *habitué* of the salon of Mme de Tencin, and at least part of his antagonism was a reflection of the generally cool, sometimes hostile attitude with which Mme de Tencin and her circle viewed Voltaire. [27]

To make matters worse, the *Epître à Uranie,* a poem that contained Voltaire's most daring attack on religion to date, had begun circulating towards the end of 1731. It scandalized an influential segment of the public and the following year the poet was obliged to placate the authorities with a denial. Voltaire then decided to vent some of his frustrations by composing a preface to *Zaïre,* part of which was fortunately omitted from publication. Nevertheless, the unexpurgated version was circulated widely enough to insure continuing ill will on the part of the Academy. Bouhier was outraged:

> Au reste, non seulement j'ai l'épître dédicatoire de *Zaïre,* telle qu'elle a été imprimée, mais on m'a encore envoyé depuis les endroits supprimés de cette épître. Ainsi, je suis en état de vous en régaler, si vous ne pouvez les recouvrer d'ailleurs.

---

[24] de Broglie, p. 195.
[25] Marais, III, 265.
[26] *Ibid.,* p. 329.
[27] For a study of Voltaire's relationship with the salon of Mme de Tencin, see Jean Sareil, *Les Tencin,* pp. 221-226 and *passim.*

> Ce qu'il y a de plus fort et de plus impertinent, ce sont des invectives grossières contre notre Académie où il dit que "le frelon prend trop souvent la place de l'abeille." Après beaucoup de belles choses pareilles, il ajoute qu'il semble que pour y avoir place, il faille être plus accablé de la risée publique qu' "honoré d'applaudissements." Enfin que "les têtes qu'on y couronne de lauriers, n'en sont pas à tel point couvertes qu'on n'y découvre encore les restes de chardons qui ceignaient leur front sacré." Ne faut-il pas avoir perdu l'esprit pour parler de la sorte?[28]

Marais concurred and expressed his indignation by return mail: "Le Voltaire est bien insolent d'avoir parlé et écrit de l'Académie comme il a fait; il se rend tous les jours indigne d'en être."[29] Furthermore, even the modified version of the preface was still far from innocuous. It contained unfavorable comments on the regime's lack of consideration for arts and letters and a tale of Mlle Lecouvreur's death and ignominious burial.

Voltaire's following publication in 1733 made a bad situation nearly hopeless. With his *Temple du goût* he succeeded in alienating even those who until then had been largely tolerant of his more unorthodox pronouncements. He was undeniably correct in many of his criticisms. What the public resented was his immodest fashion of setting himself up as a supreme judge of literature. The verdicts he handed down disposed quickly of both the dead and the living and were noticed for the striking lack of objectivity in treating the latter. His contemporaries saw themselves divided into two groups. One was condemned to scorn and ridicule; the other was obviously made up of the author's friends. The indignation Marais expressed in a letter to Bouhier probably typified the attitude of a number of Voltaire's countrymen: "L'impudence elle-même ne peut aller plus loin; il parle mal de Corneille, de Racine et de tous les autres poètes: Lamotte et Fontenelle y sont en pièces; Rousseau y est cruellement traité; Pellisson ne savoit pas écrire; on réduiroit Beyle à cinq ou six feuilles, on en trouveroit bien moins dans Marot et Rabelais; enfin ce nouveau Scioppius mord tout le monde et cherche encore des coups de bâton."[30] Among the names mentioned by Marais, that of Pellisson

---

[28] de Broglie, p. 203.
[29] Marais, III, 465.
[30] *Ibid.*, p. 472.

is of particular interest to us, since he had been the official historiographer of the French Academy. Voltaire evidently was not in a mood to flatter the organization.

Almost overnight, Voltaire had increased considerably the number of his enemies and became the target of numerous attacks. While the *Temple du goût* did not have any noticeable political repercussions for Voltaire, it created an atmosphere which was most unfavorable for him. As a result, the violent reaction occasioned by his following publication, that of the *Lettres philosophiques* in 1734, showed principally that: "Voltaire, qui savait la gravité des sujets auxquels il s'attaquait, a ... commis la faute de tactique de laisser sortir son livre au moment inopportun." [31] The events that ensued — the condemnation by the *Parlement*, the burning, the *lettre de cachet*, Voltaire's flight to Cirey, are well known and need not be examined in detail here.

Voltaire was allowed to return to Paris in March of 1735. Hérault, the Chief of Police, invited him back in the following terms:

> Son Eminence et M. le garde des sceaux m'ont chargé, monsieur, de vous mander que vous pouvez revenir à Paris lorsque vous le jugerez à propos. Ce retour a pour condition que vous vous occuperez ici d'objets qui ne donneront plus aucun sujet de former contre vous les mêmes plaintes que par le passé. Plus vous avez de talent, monsieur, plus vous devez sentir que vous avez des ennemis et des jaloux. Fermez-leur donc la bouche pour jamais par une conduite digne d'un homme sage et d'un homme qui a acquis un certain âge. [32]

These sagacious recommendations, we might add, suggested at the same time a program to be followed in seeking admission to the Academy.

The deaths of two Academicians in 1736 presented new opportunities for Voltaire. The circumstances, however, were not yet favorable, and Voltaire realized that he had to postpone his ambitions. In a letter to La Chaussée, written in May, he explained his reasons:

---

[31] Sareil, "Voltaire et le Cardinal de Fleury," p. 46.

[32] Quoted by Gustave Desnoiresterres, *Voltaire et la société au XVIIIe siècle* (Paris: Didier et Cie., 1871), II, 56-57. "Son Eminence" designates Fleury and "le garde des sceaux" was Chauvelin.

"On m'a parlé aujourd'hui d'une place à l'Académie française, mais ni les circonstances où je me trouve, ni ma santé, ni ma liberté, que je préfère à tout, ne me permettent d'oser y penser. J'ai répondu que cette place devait vous être destinée, et que je me ferais un honneur de vous céder le peu de suffrages sur lesquels j'aurais pu compter, si votre mérite ne vous assurait de toutes les voix" (Best. 1032). A number of Voltaire's contemporaries deplored this seeming unwillingness to enter the ranks of the Immortals. We have the following commentary from the anonymous author of a newssheet: "Voilà donc deux places vacantes à l'Académie française.... Les amis de Voltaire font ce qu'ils peuvent pour l'engager à faire quelques démarches pour en demander une, mais on ne peut pas plier ce cœur rebelle. Il veut qu'on la lui offre. Par cette opiniâtreté réciproque, l'académie perd un sujet digne d'elle et Voltaire un honneur qui manque à sa gloire." [33] The truth of the matter was that a realistic appraisal of the circumstances simply did not permit any hope of winning a seat. The abbé d'Olivet explained the situation to Bouhier in a letter dated 3 June 1736: "Voltaire est de retour. Il avoit grande envie de l'une des places vacantes, mais il n'a osé se mettre sur les rangs, parce que Mr. le Garde des Sceaux n'est pas encore tout à fait appaisé sur son sujet" (Best. 1044).

Two new developments even served to refresh memories. First, an article by a well known poet of the period, Jean-Baptiste Rousseau, appeared in the *Bibliothèque française* towards the middle of the year. In it, Rousseau reminisced about his meeting with Voltaire in Brussels in 1722. He recounted, for example, the following episode: "M. le comte de Lannoi ... me demanda ce que c'était qu'un jeune homme qu'il venait de voir à l'église des Sablons et qui avait tellement scandalisé tout le monde par ses indécences durant le service, que le peuple avait été sur le point de le mettre dehors." Rousseau remembered also that Voltaire had recited to him the newly composed *Epître à Julie* (also known as the *Epître à Uranie*) which seemed to him: "remplie d'horreurs contre ce que nous avons de plus saint dans la religion et contre la personne même de Jésus-Christ." Similarly, in

---

[33] Quoted by P. M. Conlon, *Voltaire's Literary Career from 1728 to 1750*, Studies on Voltaire and the Eighteenth Century, XIV (Geneva: Institut et Musée Voltaire, 1961), 213. The newssheet is a manuscript in the Bibliothèque Nationale, identified as Fonds Français 13694, f. 164.

the *Poème de la Ligue,* he found that Voltaire "s'emporte à tout propos contre l'église romaine, le pape, les prêtres séculiers et réguliers et enfin contre tous les gouvernements ecclésiastiques et politiques" (Best. 1040). It is difficult to know whether many readers were taken in by this tone of scandalized devoutness. Nevertheless, the letter did bring up matters which Voltaire wanted very much to be forgotten. He tried to justify himself in a letter that appeared in the *Bibliothèque française* on 20 September 1736, but the harm had already been done.

There was also the very unpleasant and intricate Jore affair, that dragged on for many months in 1736. This unsightly quarrel with the publisher had a very detrimental effect on Voltaire's reputation and affected his academic hopes as well. Both parties had issued *mémoires* to justify their claims, and Voltaire, with his recriminations, succeeded only in bringing more discredit upon himself:

> Voltaire est bien misérable, bien bas, il devoit sacrifier mille écus plutôt que de laisser paroître un tel *factum* contre lui . . . ; pour comble de maladresse son propre Mémoire est encor plus contre lui que celui de son Libraire. La vanité, les airs de bienfaiteurs qu'il y affecte, un certain ton d'impudence qui s'y fait sentir partout, surtout les Mensonges qu'il y avance avec tant d'effronterie sur sa pauvreté et sa générosité, tout cela fait crier contre lui. Pour le coup le voilà je pense bien loin de l'Académie, ses Amis se cachent. (Best. 1050, Le Blanc to Bouhier, 15 June 1736)

The affair was particularly injurious to Voltaire in that a certain compromising letter, which he had written to Jore, was made public and brought attention to damaging events of the past: "Cette maudite lettre faisoit tout l'embarras: c'étoit une conviction que j'étois l'auteur des *Lettres philosophiques*" (Best. 1067, Voltaire to Cideville, 2 July 1736). Yet another circumstance added to Voltaire's troubles towards this time. He had begun work on *La Pucelle* a few years earlier and segments of this scandalous work had begun circulating in 1735. They provoked an immediate reaction from the authorities; according to Condorcet, "le garde des sceaux menaça le poète d'un cul de basse-fosse, si jamais il paraissait rien de cet ouvrage" (Moland, I, 210).

In spite of this seemingly unfavorable situation, the abbé d'Olivet, who was sponsoring Voltaire's candidacy, sounded quite optimistic towards the end of the year and informed Bouhier: "M. le duc de

Richelieu et M. le duc de Villars me dirent hier qu'ils travaillaient pour lui auprès de mgr. le cardinal de Fleury et de m. le garde des sceaux, et qu'ils comptaient que moi, de mon côté, je travaillerais au-dedans de l'académie. Ainsi, selon toute apparence, voilà une élection toute faite pour la première place qui viendra à vaquer." [34] It is possible that, because of his personal bias, the abbé d'Olivet had failed to accurately estimate the extent of the hostility that faced Voltaire, both inside and outside the Academy. On the other hand, this hostility was perhaps not as intense as we might tend to imagine, and since by this time almost everyone had already adopted a set attitude towards Voltaire, the events enumerated above may not have significantly altered the favor or disfavor the poet could rely upon. A realistic appraisal of the situation could perhaps allow for some optimism. This newlygained confidence was of brief duration, however, and the hopes that may have been entertained by Voltaire and his friends were suddenly shattered by the appearance of the poem *Le Mondain*. The disappointment was all the greater since Voltaire had never anticipated such a violent reaction in writing what had seemed to be an innocent apology of an epicurean way of life. He expressed his dismay in a letter to Cideville in December 1736: "Savez-vous bien que *le Mondain* a été traité d'ouvrage scandaleux, et vous douteriez-vous qu'on eût osé prendre ce misérable prétexte pour m'accabler encore? Dans quel siècle vivons nous! et après quel siècle! Faire à un homme un crime d'avoir dit qu'Adam avait les ongles longs, et traiter cela sérieusement d'hérésie" (Best. 1166). The authorities, apparently, took these pronouncements very seriously and Voltaire was forced to flee to Holland to escape persecution.

These setbacks did not discourage Voltaire. The desire to belong to the Academy was as strong as ever. The objective was still the same, but the manner and the means to be used in attaining it had to be modified. He had learned much from his failures to win the approval of the Academy in the years '31 and '36. First, he had to be patient and allow for time to erase or to soften unpleasant impressions. It was not before 1742 that Voltaire thought it propitious to become a candidate again. By then he had grown more practical in approaching the problem of getting elected.

---

[34] Pellisson and d'Olivet, II, 434.

Around this time, Voltaire began a campaign of flattery aimed at all brokers of influence — the King, his ministers and his mistresses, members of the Academy, and finally he attempted to win over the pope himself. One of his first targets had been the minister Maurepas, but Condorcet tells us that he was not very successful. Voltaire had tried to flatter Maurepas with a poem, but "cette épître, qui renfermait autant de leçons que d'éloges, ne changea rien aux sentiments du ministre" (Moland, I, 81). The favor of Maurepas was important, but not absolutely essential. Voltaire's chances were nil, however, without the approval of the cardinal de Fleury, whose assent was considered a prerequisite for every candidacy. Voltaire's outlook in this respect suddenly improved in 1740, following the death of the King of Prussia. As a result, "Il devient une personnalité importante, non pas dans le monde littéraire, sans intérêt aux yeux de la Cour, mais sur l'échiquier politique, par le simple fait qu'il est l'ami reconnu du nouveau roi de Prusse, Frédéric II." [35] This return to favor was signaled by Voltaire's letter of 2 November 1740 to Fleury, in which he wished to set the tone of his relationship with the minister: "J'ay toujours été tendrement attaché à votre Eminence; je regarde comme un de ses bienfaits l'occasion de luy faire connoître mes vrais sentiments, mon zèle respectueux pour le roy, pour la patrie, pour la rellrigion, dont vous êtes également le père, et mon dévouement pour votre personne" (Best. 2219).

This improved situation was of short duration unfortunately, for Voltaire's position was first compromised by a letter he had written to Frederick and which was being circulated in 1742. The text of the letter alienated the Court and a good part of the public. Secondly, Voltaire decided to present his new play, *Mahomet,* on 19 August 1742, and the moment chosen for the première could hardly have been more inopportune. We have a good example of the outraged, almost hysterical reaction that followed the performance in a letter written by the *Procureur général,* Joly de Fleury, to the Chief of Police, Marville, on 13 August 1742:

> Trois personnes de ma connaissance y ont été aujourd'hui; voici ce qu'on m'a dit. C'est l'énormité en fait d'infamie, de scélératesse, d'irréligion et d'impiété, et c'est ce que disent

---

[35] Sareil, "Voltaire et le Cardinal de Fleury," p. 55.

ceux mêmes qui n'ont point de religion, "je suis étonné," disoit l'un pendant la comédie, "qu'on ne se lève pas pour faire finir la pièce," "Voilà de bonnes instructions," disoit l'autre, "pour un Ravaillac!" —"Il faudroit mettre l'auteur," a dit un autre, "à Bicêtre, pour le reste de ses jours." Un homme sortant, a trouvé son ami qui sortoit; il lui a demandé ce qu'il en pensoit. Il a répondu: "Je l'ai vue trois fois (c'est à dire la pièce)." L'autre a répliqué: "Je ne te verrai de ma vie, d'avoir eu le courage de voir trois fois de pareilles horreurs." Tout le monde dit que pour avoir composé une pareille pièce, il faut être un scélérat à faire brûler. Voilà tout ce qu'on m'a dit. C'est une révolte universelle.... On m'en a tant dit, que j'en oublie la moitié: que vous poursuivez les jansénistes et leurs écrits, et que vous laissez tranquille un auteur scélérat et qui vous fait triompher l'irréligion et les crimes.

The Chief of Police found himself in a rather delicate situation and informed the minister Maurepas: "Dussiez-vous vous moquer encore de moi, je vous dirai que l'on me mande de Paris que la pièce de *Mahomet* y fait un bruit infini, que le public en est scandalisé, et même indigné, et, par contrecoup, le lieutenant de police vilipendé." [36] Marville was finally obliged to intervene, and following the advice of Maurepas, he spoke to Voltaire, convincing him to discontinue presentation of the play. Voltaire had no choice but to comply. As he explained to Frederick: "C'est l'aventure du *Tartuffe*, — Les hypocrites persécutèrent Molière, et les fanatiques se sont soulevés contre moi. J'ai cédé au torrent sans dire un seul mot, si Socrate en eût fait autant, il n'eût point bu la ciguë" (Best. 2475, 29 August 1742).

This pragmatism was characteristic of Voltaire's actions at the time, as we have already noted. He was careful not to jeopardize the progress that he had made in his relations with the authorities. He continued courting Fleury. It was a propitious moment to be on good terms with the cardinal and the King, for a chair had just been left vacant at the Academy. The only rival for the seat was Marivaux, who also was finding it difficult to get elected. He had been rejected twice before, in 1732 and 1736, and was sponsored by Mme de Tencin, who was determined to see that her protégé was admitted

---

[36] Claude-Henri Feydeau de Marville, *Lettres au ministre Maurepas* (Paris: H. Champion, 1896), I, 60 and 63.

this time. Voltaire's candidacy was endorsed by Richelieu. In an effort to deprive Voltaire of his support, Mme de Tencin wrote the duke a letter which reveals to the reader her talent and taste for intrigue:

> Voltaire a écrit à M. de Nivernais qu'il avait le consentement du roi. Je doute que cette démarche soit de votre aveu. J'ai parlé à mes serviteurs de Dieu; ils m'ont dit que je ne pouvais trop vous représenter qu'il ne convient pas à un homme comme vous de protéger un athée; que vous aviez la réputation de parler toujours de la religion comme il convenait, et que, si vous faisiez recevoir Voltaire à l'académie, on dirait qu'il vous a perverti. [37]

The letter had the intended effect and Voltaire, once more, had to accept defeat and resign himself to waiting for a new opportunity. He did not have to wait long. The cardinal de Fleury died on 29 January 1743, and Voltaire set about providing himself with a solid backing. Through the intercession of Richelieu he won the friendship of Mme de La Tournelle, the King's latest mistress. By February he had gained the King's approval, judging from his letter to Moncrif: "Le roi m'a donné son agrément pour être de l'académie en cas qu'on veuille de moi. Reste à savoir si vous en voulez. Vous savez que pour l'honneur des lettres je veux qu'on fasse succéder un pauvre diable à un premier ministre; je me présente pour être ce pauvre diable là" (Best. 2540, 1 February 1743).

He thus tried to acquire the suffrages of a number of Academicians. The biggest opposition would obviously be set up by the members of the clergy. In a letter to d'Argental he expressed his resolve to subdue the most stubborn ones; for example: "Je ferai tout ce qu'il faudra pour apaiser, pour désarmer l'archevêque de Sens" (Best. 2541, 1 February 1743). There was also Boyer, the former Bishop of Mirepoix, who represented the most serious threat to Voltaire's chances. Boyer had acquired added influence at the death of Fleury, for he assumed the Cardinal's role of keeping out all candidates known for their impious leanings.

---

[37] *Correspondance du cardinal de Tencin, ministre d'Etat, et de Mme de Tencin, sa sœur, avec le duc de Richelieu sur les intrigues de la cour de France depuis 1742 jusqu'en 1757* (Paris: 1790), pp. 26-27.

To try to win over these stern defenders of the Church, Voltaire wrote a letter to Boyer that is remarkable for the brazenness of its allegations. His first statement is moderate, and is basically true: "Il y a longtemps, monsieur, que je suis persécuté par la calomnie et que je la pardonne." Then follows a passage that can only be understood in the light of the almost desperate nature of Voltaire's determination:

> Je peux donc dire devant dieu, qui m'écoute, que je suis bon citoyen et vrai catholique, et je le dis uniquement parceque je l'ai toujours été de cœur. Je n'ai pas écrit une page qui ne respire l'humanité, et j'en ai écrit beaucoup qui sont sanctifiées par la religion. Le poème de *La Henriade* n'est d'un bout à l'autre que l'éloge de la vertu qui se soumet à la providence; j'espère qu'en cela ma vie ressemblera toujours à mes écrits.

There was one work that everyone still remembered, which he could not explain away. He simply denied having written it: "Mes ennemis me reprochent je ne sais quelles lettres philosophiques. J'ai écrit plusieurs lettres à mes amis, mais jamais je ne les ai intitulées de ce titre fastueux. La plupart de celles qu'on a imprimées sous mon nom ne sont point de moi, et j'ai des preuves qui le démontrent" (Best. 2543, February 1743). Voltaire made the letter available to the public, but it is hardly surprising that it did not really convince anyone. The duc de Luynes noted on 3 March 1743: "Il paraît depuis quelques jours une lettre de Voltaire écrite à un ami. Quoiqu'elle soit très-bien écrite, il y a lieu de croire qu'elle ne fera changer de sentiment personne." [38]

A letter similar in content and in purpose was written to another Academician, the abbé de Saint-Cyr. Voltaire repeated the same assertions, that only a few of the works published under his name were really his and suggested the reasons for which he should be accepted:

> Mes sentiments véritables sur ce qui peut regarder l'état et la religion, tout inutiles qu'ils sont étaient bien connus en dernier lieu de feu M. le cardinal de Fleury, il m'a fait

---

[38] Charles-Philippe d'Albert de Luynes, *Mémoires du duc de Luynes sur la cour de Louis XV (1735-1758)*, ed. M. L. Dussieux and E. Soulié (Paris: Didot, 1860-1865), IV, 424.

> l'honneur de m'écrire dans les derniers temps de sa vie, vingt lettres qui prouvent assez que le fond de mon cœur ne lui déplaisait pas. Il a daigné faire passer jusqu'au roi même un peu de cette bonté dont il m'honorait. Ces raisons seraient mon excuse si j'osais demander dans la république des lettres la place de ce sage ministre. (Best. 2544, February 1743)

An event that took place a month before the election seemed to improve further Voltaire's prospects for victory. On 20 February 1743, the première of *Mérope* was held and proved to be one of the greatest all-time successes of the French theater. On the following day, the abbé de Bernis wrote enthusiastically to Voltaire: "L'Académie vous recevra, Monsieur, quand il lui plaira. Toute la France assemblée vous rendit hier un hommage qu'elle réserve toujours pour les grands hommes" (Best. 2548).

In reality, however, there was little ground to be optimistic. Voltaire had not taken into account several factors that would influence the Academy's decision. First of all, the friendship of Mme de La Tournelle (who was to become the duchess of Châteauroux later that year) actually rendered him a disservice. She was the declared enemy of Maurepas, and the latter found this to be an excellent occasion to take unobtrusive revenge on the King's favorite. The following account of a meeting between the writer and the minister is given in Voltaire's *Mémoires,* written some sixteen years later:

> J'allai trouver ce ministre; je lui dis: "Une place à l'académie n'est pas une dignité bien importante; mais, après avoir été nommé, il est triste d'être exclu! Vous êtes brouillé avec Mme de Châteauroux, que le roi aime, et avec M. le duc de Richelieu, qui la gouverne; quel rapport y a-t-il, je vous prie, de vos brouilleries avec une pauvre place à l'Académie française? Je vous conjure de me répondre franchement; en cas que Mme de Châteauroux l'emporte sur M. l'évêque de Mirepoix, vous y opposerez-vous?... "Il se recueillit un moment et me dit: "Oui, et je vous écraserai."

Maurepas formed an alliance with Boyer, who is remembered with a good amount of bitterness in the *Mémoires*: "Un vieil imbécile, précepteur du dauphin, autrefois théatin, et depuis évêque de Mirepoix, nommé Boyer, se chargea, par principe de conscience, de seconder le caprice de M. de Maurepas.... Il représenta que c'était offenser Dieu qu'un profane comme moi succédât à un cardinal" (Moland, I, 24).

Voltaire had underestimated the intensity of the hatred shared by Boyer's faction. They were almost desperate in their efforts to keep the "coryphée de l'irréligion" out of their body. A recently published letter from dom La Taste, bishop of Bathleem, written on 2 February 1743 to Boyer, shows the resolve and the intense hostility of the party opposing Voltaire's candidacy:

> De toutes parts j'entends murmurer de ce que M. Voltaire s'est mis sur les rangs pour obtenir de l'Académie française la place vacante par la mort de Monseigneur le cardinal de Fleury; et, ce qui afflige le plus, c'est qu'il se dit favorisé du Roi pour la recherche de cette place.... M. Voltaire est encore *in reatu*; un arrêt, dont il ne s'est jamais lavé, a condamné aux flammes ses *Lettres philosophiques,* remplies de l'esprit séditieux et de l'irréligion des Anglais. L'impie *Lettre à Uranie* dont le public persiste à le charger, et ses discours libertins qui ont corrompu tant de femmes et de jeunes gens, l'ont rendu abominable aux personnes qui connaissent et respectent la Religion: et ce sera un tel homme qui paraîtra aux yeux de tout le Royaume muni de la protection de Sa Majesté!... On dit que ce qui fait pencher le Roi pour ce choix, c'est que personne n'est plus capable que Voltaire de répandre sur les cendres de Monseigneur le cardinal de Fleury les fleurs que ce digne ministre mérite. Mais un prélat si religieux pendant sa vie et à la mort peut-il être loué convenablement par une bouche accoutumée au blasphème? Je suis persuadé que s'il pouvait revivre un moment, il en rougirait, et qu'il supplierait Sa Majesté de ne pas imprimer à sa mémoire cette tache, qu'un Voltaire succède à un cardinal de Fleury. [39]

The opposition's efforts were successful. The Bishop of Mirepoix and his supporters carried the day: the King was finally convinced that a heretic should not succeed the cardinal. One small problem remained — Boyer's clan had to find a suitable candidate for the vacancy and Voltaire's friends had taken care to dissuade any potential applicants: "Nous espérions prendre la place par famine" (Best. 2585, Mme Du Châtelet to the abbé de Sade, June 1743). The solution was found

---

[39] Jean Sareil, "Quelques Lettres de Voltaire et de ses amis," *Revue d'Histoire littéraire de la France,* IV (July-August 1970), 657-658.

in the person of Albert de Luynes, Bishop of Bayeux, a few days before the election was to take place. The story of this improvisation was recorded by the candidate's brother, the duke of Luynes:

> Hier, M. Hardion, directeur de l'Académie, rendit compte au Roi de l'élection, faite jeudi dernier, de mon frère pour remplir la place vacante par la mort de M. le cardinal de Fleury.... Mon frère ne songeait en aucune manière à cette place. Etant allé rendre visite à M. de Maurepas, sans aucun dessein de lui en parler, M. de Maurepas lui en parla le premier, et lui dit qu'il devroit y songer; que cette demande seroit bien reçue. Mon frère en parla à M. l'évêque de Mirepoix qui est fort de nos amis et qui est de l'Académie. M. de Mirepoix lui parla de la même manière que M. de Maurepas, et en rendit compte au Roi, qui parut approuver que mon frère fît les démarches nécessaires. En conséquence, mon frère alla chez tous les académiciens, et jeudi fut élu tout d'une voix.[40]

For the first time in these long years of struggling to conquer an Academic chair, we see Voltaire giving in to discouragement. On 1 April 1743, he confided to his friend d'Argental: "Si j'étais plus jeune et moins persécuté, je travaillerais encore. Je suis venu dans le temps de la barbarie. Je ne sais rien de cette Académie. Tout ce que je sais, c'est qu'il est bien cruel que deux hommes puissants se soient réunis pour m'arracher un agrément frivole, la seule récompense que je demandais après trente années de travail" (Best. 2562). In another letter, written a few days later, he stated: "Je crois qu'il convient à un profane comme moy de renoncer pour jamais à l'Académie" (Best. 2563, to d'Aigueberre, 4 April 1743). He did not mean it. The dejection was short-lived; Voltaire soon rebounded from this disappointment and renewed his campaign. His failure had not been in vain, for he had learned certain valuable lessons from it and would shape his actions accordingly from now on. He was going to work harder than ever at rehabilitating his image.

The general impression left by the events of March 1743 was that Voltaire had fallen into total disrepute. The ever-present pamphleteers only served to reinforce these appearances. In reality, this impression of disfavor was only cultivated by the government in view

---

[40] Luynes, IV, 452.

of a secret mission that Voltaire had been given. He was asked to visit the King of Prussia in order to find out his intentions in the sphere of European politics. The recent events provided an excellent camouflage for this enterprise. As Voltaire recounts: "Il fallait un prétexte. Je pris celui de ma querelle avec l'ancien évêque de Mirepoix. Le roi approuva cet expédient. J'écrivis au roi de Prusse que je ne pouvais plus tenir aux persécutions de ce théatin, et que j'allais me réfugier auprès d'un roi philosophe, loin des tracasseries d'un bigot" (Moland, I, 25). Frederick soon discovered the real motives for Voltaire's visit. Nevertheless, he thoroughly enjoyed the company of the greatest writer of France. For Voltaire, the stay in Potsdam was pleasant enough, but did not bring any concrete results. His trip, however, had achieved one essential goal: "Il y a tout lieu de penser que la réconciliation entre la France et la Prusse a été avancée dans les soupers de Potsdam entre des louanges à la poésie et des attaques contre la religion."[41] Satisfied with his beginnings in politics, Voltaire returned to France in November 1743 and began looking for new ways in which to serve the government.

With the exception of one setback (the censor's interdiction halting the production of *Jules César* in 1743) it can be said that the period extending from his candidacy of 1743 until his election in 1746 witnesses a remarkable improvement in the relations between Voltaire and the authorities. His friends helped him greatly by providing him with opportunities to flatter the King and other persons of distinction. Thus, in 1744, at the suggestion of Richelieu, he began the text for a musical divertissement, *La Princesse de Navarre*, to help celebrate the Dauphin's marriage to Marie-Thérèse of Spain. Towards the end of the year he wrote also his poem on the *Evénements de l'année 1744*, praising the reign of Louis XV. Voltaire was principally interested in gaining the King's favor, and seeing that recompense for his efforts was slow in coming he enlisted the help of his friend d'Argenson, who was then Minister of Foreign Affairs: "La charge de gentil-homme ordinaire ne vaquant presque jamais, et cet agrément n'étant qu'un agrément, on y peut ajouter la petite place d'historiographe" (Best. 2856, 8 February 1745). Voltaire was granted his two wishes and showed his appreciation and his continued desire to please

---

[41] Sareil, *Les Tencin*, 353. For a detailed account and evaluation of Voltaire's mission, see pp. 351-375.

with additional literary flatteries. The victory of Fontenoy gave him the opportunity to compose a poem that was a masterpiece of the genre, if we judge by the success it achieved with a majority of the public and with the principal heroes of the battle, whose exploits had been so cleverly put into verse. "Ce poème faisait de Voltaire un poète national," [42] and he was again recompensed with a special mark of distinction from the King and was congratulated by Maurepas: "Le roi vient de vous accorder, monsieur, la médaille que s.m. avait fait frapper à l'occasion de la journée de Fontenoy. Cette faveur convenait parfaitement à celui qui a si dignement célébré cette victoire. Je suis charmé, en vous l'envoyant, de pouvoir vous féliciter sur cette marque de bonté que s.m. vous donne" (Best. 2999, 7 November 1745). Complying with one more special request issued by Richelieu, Voltaire wrote the *Temple de la Gloire* to be performed in honor of the King. A few months later, yet another glorifying spectacle, *Les Fêtes de Ramire,* was begun.

Indeed, Voltaire was enjoying unprecedented favor at the court. He had, in addition, the friendship of the marquise de Pompadour and in his memoirs ascribes the greatest part of his success to his relationship with the King's mistress:

> Je passai quelques mois avec elle à Etiole, pendant que le roi faisait la campagne de 1746. Cela me valut des récompenses qu'on n'avait jamais données ni à mes ouvrages ni à mes services. Je fus jugé digne d'être l'un des quarante membres inutiles de l'académie. Je fus nommé historiographe de France; et le roi me fit présent d'une charge de gentilhomme ordinaire de sa chambre. Je conclus que, pour faire la plus petite fortune, il valait mieux dire quatre mots à la maîtresse d'un roi que d'écrire cent volumes. (Moland, I, 33-34) [43]

---

[42] André Bellessort, *Essai sur Voltaire* (Paris: Perrin, 1950), p. 154.

[43] Voltaire fails to mention the duke of Richelieu, who was also instrumental in influencing the King. It is impossible to determine who helped most to convince the King, but the friendship of the King's favorite was certainly not detrimental to Voltaire's cause. Mr. Conlon, nonetheless, takes the extreme position of assigning all of the credit to Richelieu (Conlon, p. 222), and argues that the duke alone had won the King's acquiescence in 1743. The King, however, changed his mind in 1743, just before the election, showing that Richelieu's influence was not enough then and could have proven insufficient in 1746 as well.

Voltaire had learned, however, that the King's approval alone was not sufficient. At this same time, while assiduously courting Louis XV, he had put into motion an elaborate plan destined to win the good graces of the pope himself. Voltaire had already been entertaining this project for several years and had conceived the idea following the forced closing of his play *Mahomet*. On 22 August 1742, he had declared to d'Argental: "Puisque me voilà la victime des jansénistes, je dédierai *Mahomet* au pape, et je compte être évêque *in partibus infidelium* attendu que c'est là mon véritable diocèse" (Best. 2471). A year later, while on his way to meet Frederick, he made his intentions known to Cideville:

> Je veux en partant de Berlin
> Demander justice au Saint Père
> J'iray baiser son pied divin
> Et chez vous je viendrai soudain
> Avec indulgence plénière,
> Car Le Sage Lambertini
> N'est point cagot atrabilaire:
> Il est rempli de la lumière
> Di questi grandi romani
> Admirez! de la terre entière,
> Des beaux arts il est deffenseur
> Et le successeur de Saint Pierre
> De Leon dix est successeur.
> Je veux avoir enfin Rome pour mon amie
> Et malgré quelques vers hardis
> Je veux être un Elu dans le Saint paradis
> Si je suis réprouvé dans votre académie.
>   (Best. 2593, 27 June 1743)

The thought was presented half jestingly, but it was not long before Voltaire began carrying it out. The plan was not without daring, but it was to Voltaire's credit that he had conceived it. The triumph of his election to the Academy in 1746 most certainly hinged on this successful negotiation with the pope, which completely disarmed the opposition of the *dévots* inside the Academy. The circumstances governing this "truly Voltairean procedure" [44] were highly favorable because the pope, Benedict XIV, was a true representative of the eight-

---

[44] Albert Bachman, *Censorship in France from 1715 to 1750* (New York: Institute of French Studies, Columbia Univ., 1934), p. 113.

eenth century; he was indeed an enlightened pope and "had adapted himself... to the spirit of the age." [45] Historian Pierre Lanfrey characterizes him as "un homme doux, tolérant, modéré, plein de sagesse et de philosophie." [46] Voltaire appreciated these qualities of "Le Sage Lambertini" as we can see from his letter to Cideville.

Voltaire could not present his amazing request directly. Therefore he would have recourse once more to the intermediation of his friends. He addressed himself to the marquis d'Argenson, asking him to convince the abbé de Canillac, the French *chargé d'affaires* at the court of Rome, to intercede in his favor. The minister must have taken rather sceptically this strange petition, for a short time later Voltaire insisted: "Vous avez eu trop de scrupule en craignant d'écrire un petit mot à M. l'abbé de Canillac. Je vous avertis que je suis très bien avec le Pape, et que M. l'abbé de Canillac fera sa cour en disant au saint-père que je lis ses ouvrages, et que je suis au rang de ses admirateurs comme de ses brebis. Chargez-vous, je vous en supplie, de cette importante négociation" (Best. 2884, 3 May 1745).

Rather than await the outcome of this first negotiation, Voltaire launched a second probe. He requested the assistance of a certain Mlle du Thil, who was a friend of Mme Du Châtelet and knew the abbé de Tolignan at the court of Rome. The abbé de Tolignan complied and presented Voltaire's play and homages to the pontiff. But so much zeal almost backfired. No sooner had the pope given Tolignan two of his medals as an indication of his good will toward Voltaire than the abbé de Canillac entered with a strangely familiar request. The pope evidently was a man with a sense of humor, for instead of revealing to Canillac the repetitive nature of the latter's mission, he sent him off without medals, but with the promise that "à la Saint-Pierre il en aura de plus grosses" (Best. 2900, Voltaire to d'Argenson, 30 May 1745). At Voltaire's request the marquis d'Argenson intervened in time to prevent any misunderstandings between the two diplomatic missions. The philosophe thanked the minister in his usual style: "Je vous remercie de ces deux faces de pontife, du

---

[45] Ludwig Pastor, *The History of the Popes from the Close of the Middle Ages*, trans. E. F. Peeler & Frederick I. Antrobus (London: K. Paul, Trench, Trubner, 1938-1968), XXXVI, 134.

[46] Pierre Lanfrey, *Histoire politique des papes* (Paris: Charpentier, 1880), p. 379.

meilleur de mon cœur; je crois que sans vous, ces deux visages là qu'on m'envoyait, se seraient en allés en brouet d'andouille. L'abbé de Tolignan, le cardinal Aquaviva, l'abbé de Canillac, ne se seraient point entendus pour me faire avoir les bénédictions papales, si vous n'aviez eu la bonté d'écrire" (Best. 2945, 10 August 1745). He ended the letter with a practical recommendation: "Vous devriez bien dire au roi très chrétien combien je suis un sujet très chrétien." These diplomatic successes were obviously without value to Voltaire if they were not publicized and made known to certain important parties. The fortunate outcome of these negotiations encouraged Voltaire to address himself directly to Benedict XIV in order to further consolidate the good graces of the pontiff. He asked for permission to dedicate his *Mahomet* to the pope in a letter that is most humble and respectful in tone: "Your Holiness will kindly forgive the audacity shown by one of the humblest followers, but one of the greatest admirers of virtue in dedicating to the head of the true religion, a work directed against the founder of a false and barbarous sect" (Best. 2949, 17 August 1745).[47] Similar compliments and pledges of allegiance were expressed in a second letter written the same day (Best. 2950).

At the same time, Voltaire was also maintaining an active correspondence with some of the higher Vatican prelates and a few of the more influential Italian personalities who were to put in an occasional good word for him. On 17 August, for example, he asked Leprotti, the pope's physician and intimate friend, to let the pontiff know that Voltaire was "just as devoted to his service as he was an admirer of all his eminent qualities" (Best. 2951, 17 August 1745).

The pope reacted very graciously to this campaign of flattery and honored Voltaire with a most courteous, almost cordial letter: "We duly thank you for the unusual kindness you have shown us, assuring you that we have the greatest esteem for your recognized worth in the field of letters" (Best. 2967, 15 September 1745). Voltaire responded with another well-turned compliment expressing his "most humble thanks" (Best. 2980). At the same time, he did not forget the practical side of these transactions and immediately sought to publicize the new aura of respectability that he had gained from his correspondence with the pope. Voltaire explained to d'Argental: "Vraiment,

---

[47] The translations from Italian into English of Voltaire's correspondence with the pope and with Leprotti are mine.

les grâces célestes ne peuvent trop se répandre, et la lettre du saint père est faite pour être publique. Il est bon, mon respectable ami, que les persécuteurs des gens de bien sachent que je suis couvert contre eux de l'étole du vicaire de Dieu" (Best. 2978, 5 October 1745).

Understandably enough, the exchange of these civilities was not approved of in some quarters, and more than a year later the pope was still being reproached for his indulgence: "Tous les Bons catholiques de France ont appris avec une extrême douleur que Votre Sainteté avoit envoyé à l'infâme Athée Arrouet de Voltaire deux médailles d'or, comme une marque de protection et de la bienveillance dont Votre Sainteté daigne l'honorer" (Best. 3138, Louzeau to Pope Benedict XIV, 7 October 1746).

Those who were not scandalized by the pope's attitude with regard to Voltaire were at least surprised. The pontiff's singular indulgence was motivated in part, as we have seen, by his extremely tolerant and understanding nature. He had, in addition, a genuine interest in literature and a predilection for men of letters. Contrary to the existing public opinion, he was never deceived by Voltaire's profession of devoutness. Voltaire realized this full well himself. He had written to d'Argenson on 10 August: "Je viens, monseigneur, de recevoir le portrait du plus joufflu saint père que nous avons eu depuis longtemps. Il a l'air d'un bon diable et d'un homme qui sait à peu près ce que tout cela vaut" (Best. 2945). We gain a deeper insight into the considerations that motivated Benedict XIV from the letters he wrote to the Cardinal de Tencin. These explanations are especially interesting since they were apparently intended for a larger public as well: his correspondance with Tencin "a l'importance d'une correspondance officielle."[48] Benedict XIV gave the following account of his dealings with Voltaire in a letter dated 9 February 1746:

> Concerning the matter that has been exaggerated by Voltaire, the story is as follows. Cardinal Aquaviva was the one who showed us his tragedy with a letter of his, and we believe that he did it upon the request of the abbé de Tolignan, his intimate friend, to whom, we felt, we had to deny access to us after the first visit. The letter was full of very respectful feelings toward the Holy See and the Church. Since we are not aware that the author is recognized as

---

[48] Sareil, *Les Tencin*, p. 303.

> being outside our communion, we deemed it proper to answer him and the answer was conceived following the guideline of St. Jerome, who, when reproached for having praised and exalted Originus, wrote "we praise the philosopher, not the dogmatist." ... This is the whole sequence of this exaggerated affair. We try not to do wrong, as for the rest, we care little about unfounded gossip.[49]

Benedict XIV also explained that he had forbidden both the printing and the staging of *Mahomet* in Rome. Thus, while showing the greatest consideration for the author, he appreciated well enough the potentially subversive nature of his works.

Perhaps as a result of criticisms directed against his actions, the pope found it necessary, a few months later, to explain his stand more fully. On 13 April 1746 he referred again to Voltaire:

> It cannot be denied that he has a great sense of humor, that he is a very bright and learned man, and if he were not all for Us, which we really do not believe, it would be justifiable to flatter him, so that he might become all Ours, inasmuch as the Church and the Holy See have suffered considerable damage from persons who have been driven away, persons who, had they stayed with us, would not have done later the harm they did.[50]

This conciliatory attitude espoused by the pope was also shared by a few Jesuits, Voltaire's former teachers, and was responsible to a large degree for Voltaire's successful election in 1746. A conscious effort was being made to salvage whatever was left from Voltaire's good will towards the Church and to at least preserve appearances. The official publication of the Jesuits, the *Mémoires pour l'histoire des sciences et des beaux-arts* (also known as the *Journal de Trévoux*), had already evinced this type of attitude for some time: "The editors of the *Journal* sought to foster the friendly relations enjoyed with Voltaire and, ignoring his irreligious writings, praised his literary production liberally in the hope that the errant philosopher would not

---

[49] Emilia Morelli, ed., *La Lettere di Benedetto XIV al Card. de Tencin* (Rome: Edizioni di Storia e Letteratura, 1955), pp. 314-315. My translation.
[50] *Ibid.*, p. 331. My translation.

drift further away from his religion." [51] It must also be added that the distinctly anti-Jansenistic tone of works such as the *Lettres philosophiques* and *Mahomet* accounted for some of the consideration Voltaire enjoyed in the eyes of the Jesuits.

The Jesuit-Jansenist conflict provided Voltaire with additional opportunities to assure himself of supporters. The Jansenists had attacked him in their clandestine publication, *Les Nouvelles Ecclésiastiques*. In January of 1746, they condemned vehemently the pope's liberality in his dealings with the philosopher:

> Sa sainteté Ecrit à son cher fils le Sr de Voltaire un Bref de Compliment sur sa Belle Tragédie de Mahomet; Tragédie que le Ministre public a deffendu de Représenter sur le Théâtre français. Au Bref Etonnant le St Pere joint des médailles d'or pour témoigner au Poète l'estime qu'il fait de ses talents. L'auteur des lettres Philosophiques brulées par la main du Bourreau, "Lettres" dont l'impiété a soulevé tous ceux qui ont encore quelque religion — cet auteur en commerce avec le Pape, tandis que des Evêques, des Prêtres, des Religieux... sont traités d'excommuniés! Y a-t-il encore de la foi sur la terre: Et tout n'annonce-t-il pas que la Vérité se retire, et nous abandonne? [52]

On 1 April 1746, Voltaire wrote a long letter to Father de la Tour, principal of the Jesuit college Louis-le-Grand, presenting himself as a victim of the Jansenists and disavowing his most compromising works. He denounced the "Convulsionnaires" and their practices and swore eternal allegiance to his former masters, "ceux qui m'ont inspiré le goût des Belles lettres et des sentiments qui seront jusqu'au Tombeau la Consolation de ma Vie." The high point of the letter is a passage which, of all the palinodes that Voltaire ever indulged in, is probably the most striking one. He declared to his accusers that "si jamais on a imprimé sous mon Nom une page qui puisse scandaliser seulement le sacristain de leur paroisse je suis prêt de la déchirer... je Veux Vivre et Mourir Tranquillement dans le sein de l'Eglise Catholique, Apostolique et Romaine sans attaquer personne, sans nuire

---

[51] John N. Pappas, *The Journal de Trévoux and the Philosophes*, Studies on Voltaire and the Eighteenth Century, III (Geneva: Institut et Musée Voltaire, 1957), 87.

[52] *Les Nouvelles Ecclésiastiques*, 1 January 1746, p. 3.

à personne, sans sentir la moindre opinion qui puisse offenser personne" (Best. 3044).

Simon de la Tour accepted Voltaire's statements at their face value, and his courteous reply of 5 April expressed his appreciation and gratitude for Voltaire's newly-found piety (Best. 3045). The two letters were made public and were immediately attacked by the Jansenists, who denounced Voltaire for his flagrant hypocrisy and Simon de la Tour for his naïve credulity.[53] In reality, Father de la Tour was not fooled, but he certainly was flattered. Moreover, the Jesuits were only too happy to accept the solidarity of this staunch and talented enemy of the Jansenists.

It mattered little that the public had not been misled by Voltaire's allegations; appearances had been preserved and this boost to the philosophe's public image came at an opportune moment. A new vacancy had just occured at the Academy, following the death of Bouhier on 17 March, and Voltaire was organizing a new campaign. His letter to Father de la Tour had been written to prepare the assault.[54] Afraid of experiencing a new disappointment, Voltaire had enlisted the help of his friends. He had written to d'Argental in March and had stated his reticence: "On a parlé déjà à V. de la succession dans la partie de fumée qu'avait à Paris ledit président commentateur. V. est malade, V. n'est guère en état de se donner du mouvement, V. grisonne et ne peut pas honnêtement frapper aux portes, quoiqu'il compte sur l'agrément du roi. Il remercie tendrement ses adorables anges. Il sera très flatté d'être désiré, mais il craindra toujours de faire des démarches" (Best. 3038). Voltaire then proceeded

---

[53] *Ibid.*, 1 May 1746, p. 69.
[54] Theodore Besterman finds that although "universally accepted," it has not been proven that Voltaire wrote to Father La Tour in order to facilitate his election to the Academy. He agrees, however, that it is plausible (Best. XV, 41). This thesis has been found valid here because there are several circumstances that point toward the correctness of the theory. First of all, this letter fits perfectly into Voltaire's customary scheme of preparations for a candidacy. Secondly, two days after receiving a reply from Father La Tour, Voltaire began corresponding with Moncrif in order to elicit the academician's support. Thus, on 7 April he assured Moncrif that he had the backing of the Jesuits, since he now had Father La Tour's letter of 5 April to substantiate his claims. Voltaire had the Academy very much on his mind at the time, and it is highly unlikely that the thought of using an eventual blessing from the principal of his former school had not occurred to him before he wrote to La Tour on 1 April.

to solicit the suffrages and the helpful influence of a few Academicians whom he could regard as his friends. On 9 April, he wrote to Destouches: "Il s'agit, mon cher Terence, de faire le bonheur de ma vie, de me nommer votre confrère" (Best. 3048). He received also the help of Moncrif, who had some influence in several important circles. On 7 April, Voltaire wrote: "Je vous remercie bien davantage de votre conversation avec le père Perrussau" (Best. 3047), and on 15 April: "Aimable silphe je sçai toutes les faveurs célestes que vous m'avez faites dans votre moyenne région" (Best. 3035). [55] He turned to Moncrif for protection upon the occasion of renewed defamatory attacks by his old enemy, Roy. Hearing that Voltaire was again a candidate for a vacancy at the Academy, the pamphleteer had written a *Discours prononcé à la porte de l'académie française, par M. le directeur, à M****. Voltaire tried to turn the event to his advantage: "Je pense que cette satire vaut une recommandation, et que vos confrères n'en seront que plus affermis dans leurs bontez pour moy. Ils ne soufriront pas que ce scélérat les fasse rougir de leur choix!" He suggested that Roy's attacks would serve as an argument to influence the Queen herself: "Mais comment la plus vertueuse de toutes les reines peut elle soufrir quelquefois le plus scélérat des hommes? Je vous le diray hardiment, vous vous rendez coupable si vous ne représentez pas à sa majesté la vérité" (Best. 3053). One day later Voltaire presented similar reasoning to the Academician Alary. Speaking of Roy's calumnies, he wrote: "J'ose souhaiter L'unanimité des suffrages pour réponse à cette infamie. Ce sera là sa première punition" (Best. 3055). He then addressed himself to Moncrif again: "J'ose croire que M. l'abbé de St. Cir ira à L'académie le jour de L'élection, et qu'il ne me refusera pas ce beau titre d'élu" (Best. 3057, 20 April 1746).

All of this frantic activity, coupled with the efforts of Voltaire's friends, was apparently bringing results, for on 16 April the marquis d'Argenson was announcing to Voltaire "Je sçays combien votre jettonnerie est sûre" (Best. 3054). There was still, however, one major obstacle on the road to the Academy. Duclos, a second, very powerful candidate, was presenting himself for the vacant seat. Fortunately,

---

[55] Pérusseau was the King's confessor. The "moyenne région" may refer to the Queen's entourage, where Moncrif had considerable influence.

Duclos stepped aside, out of deference for Voltaire, his senior and his superior in the field of letters.

The meeting to choose the candidate took place on 25 April, and the minutes for that day were recorded as follows: "La Compagnie au nombre de 29 s'étant assemblée aujourd'hui pour proposer un Académicien à la place de feu M. le Président Bouhier, Mons. de Voltaire a eu la pluralité des voix" (Registres, II, 586). The King's assent had been obtained: "Le Roi avait parlé et même fait écrire qu'il ne s'opposerait point à son élection." [56] Voltaire was duly elected on 2 May: "Le Roi ayant agréé la proposition qui lui a été faite de Mr. de Voltaire pour succéder à Mr. le Président Bouhier, la Compagnie a procédé aujourd'hui au second scrutin qui a été encore favorable à Mr. de Voltaire, et son élection a été confirmée" (Registres, II, 586). Voltaire thus became the seventh member to occupy the twelfth chair of the French Academy.

---

[56] Luynes, VII, 293.

Chapter II

THE "NEGLECTED" ACADEMY

On Monday, 9 May 1746, Voltaire pronounced his inaugural address. The event attracted a good amount of attention and the editor of the *Journal de Trévoux* commented: "M. de Voltaire se présente à l'Académie Française, et m. l'abbé d'Olivet est son introducteur. Cela doit faire une époque dans l'histoire de cette compagnie, et les discours de l'un et de l'autre seront des monuments." [1] The ceremony was well attended, according to the *Mercure de France*: "Le public qui court toujours en foule aux assemblées de l'Académie sembloit avoir redoublé d'empressement pour celle-ci; les raisons de cet empressement sont connues de toute l'Europe avec les ouvrages de M. de Voltaire, et l'assemblée qui avoit droit d'attendre de ce grand homme un discours brillant n'a pas été trompée dans son attente." [2] Voltaire's discourse proved indeed to be worthy of attention and successfully broke the mold of the traditional and banal harangue. It was not possible, of course, to dispense altogether with the usual platitudes. He did succeed, however, in being convincingly eloquent in voicing the praises of the first protectors of the Academy: "Il en est de ces éloges qu'on répète comme de ces solennités qui sont toujours les mêmes, et qui réveillent la mémoire des événements chers à un peuple entier: elles sont nécessaires. Célébrer des hommes tels que le cardinal de Richelieu, Louis XIV, un Séguier, un Colbert, un Turenne, un Condé, c'est dire à haute voix: "Rois, ministres, généraux à venir, imitez ces grands hommes" (Moland, XXIII, 215). The central part

---

[1] *Mémoires pour l'histoire des sciences et des beaux-arts,* June 1746, p. 1339.

[2] *Mercure de France,* June 1746, p. 48.

of Voltaire's discourse examined the history of the French language and considered briefly the authors, past and present, who had contributed most to its beauties and richness. Among the living, Voltaire paid homage to Crébillon, Fontenelle, the abbé d'Olivet, Hénault, Montesquieu, and to his young protégé, Vauvenargues. The principal theme of the speech was the universality of the French language, and in examining the qualifications the French possessed for this distinction, Voltaire sounded a note of warning: "J'avoue que la gloire de nos armes se soutient mieux que celle de nos lettres" (Moland, XXIII, 213). Yet he was hopeful that the prestige his language had enjoyed in the past would not seriously diminish, for "le feu qui nous éclairait n'est pas encore éteint" (Moland, XXIII, 215). Voltaire's discourse had already been modified and its scope restricted by a panel of Academicians who had reviewed it before the day of inauguration: "Ils exigèrent absolument que je me renfermasse dans les objets de littérature qui sont du ressort de L'académie, et retranchèrent tout ce qui paroissoit s'en écarter" (Best. 3113, Voltaire to Maupertuis, 3 July 1746). It managed, nevertheless, to include tributes addressed to some of the most eminent Francophiles in Europe: the King of Prussia, his sister, who was the Queen of Sweden, Pope Benedict XIV, Peter the Great and his daughter. The new Academician did not forget to mention his "hero" Richelieu, and ended with the customary homage to the King, Louis XV.

The speech was in general very well received. The *Mercure de France* noted that "il fut souvent interrompu par les applaudissements du public frappé des traits brillants dont ce discours est semé." [3] Copies of the discourse quickly reached the provinces, where it often met with a favorable reaction, as we can see in a letter of the *président* de Brosses:

> Je ne sais ce qu'on aura dit et pensé à Paris du discours de Voltaire; pour moi, je vous avouerai naturellement qu'il m'a fait un très grand plaisir... toute la partie de son discours qui roule sur les causes du progrès de la langue et de la décadence actuelle du goût, m'a paru également vraie, juste, sensée, bien écrite. On dit que ce n'était pas sa place, mais moi je trouverais, au contraire, que rien n'est mieux placé dans un discours académique, et que cela vaut mieux qu'une

---

[3] *Ibid.*, p. 61.

perpétuelle monotonie d'éloges rebattus. Enfin, il me semble que ce discours est un des meilleurs que j'aie lus. (Best. 3097, de Brosses to de Gemeaux, 4 June 1746)

The originality of Voltaire's speech had apparently raised a slight controversy. Remembering his inauguration some thirty years later in the *Commentaire historique,* where he refers to himself in the third person, Voltaire showed considerable pride for having played this innovative role: "Il fut le premier qui dérogea à l'usage fastidieux de ne remplir un discours de réception que des louanges rebattues du cardinal de Richelieu. Il releva sa harangue par des remarques nouvelles sur la langue française et sur le goût. Ceux qui ont été reçus après lui ont, pour la plupart, suivi et perfectionné cette méthode utile" (Moland, I, 91). It must be noted that Voltaire was not the first Academician to depart from the accepted form of inaugural address. Bossuet, La Bruyère, and Fontenelle had done it before him.[4] Nevertheless, Voltaire's example had a greater impact, for following his inauguration most of the writers admitted to the Academy began treating similar topics in their first official speeches. In 1754, Grimm noticed with a certain amount of surprise that these discourses were beginning to interest the public.[5]

Voltaire was not permitted the full enjoyment of this long-sought moment of glory. Defamatory attacks had started already before he was elected to the Academy.[6] Upon his election several other pamphlets appeared. There was a *Discours prononcé à l'Académie par M. de Voltaire,* an ironic harangue by a certain Baillet de Saint-Julien; a *Lettre d'un académicien de Villefranche à M. de Voltaire,* and *Réflexions sur le remerciement de M. de V. à l'Académie française.*[7] Stung by this succession of satires, Voltaire initiated a series of complaints and charges directed against the authors and the sellers and distributors of the pamphlets. These various litigations and

---

[4] Conlon, p. 225.
[5] Friedrich Melchior von Grimm, *Correspondance littéraire, philosophique et critique par Grimm, Diderot, Raynal, Meister, Etc.,* ed. Maurice Tourneux (Paris: 1877-1882), II, 360 and 457.
[6] When Roy had reissued his satire, see above, p. 49.
[7] Roy's *Discours,* the *Réflexions sur le remerciement...,* and other satiric pieces were published anonymously by Travenol and Mannory in 1748, in a volume entitled *Voltariana ou éloges amphigouriques de Fr. Marie Arrouet.*

pursuits embittered Voltaire's existence over a period of several months in the middle of 1746.

In the meantime, he was taking seriously his academic responsibilities and assiduously attending the Academy's meetings. In the four months following his election, Voltaire was present at twenty three such gatherings. The Academy met three times a week, and more often than not, Voltaire was present at two of the meetings (Registres, II, 587-594). He took part also in the Academy's official ceremonies. On 22 July 1746, he joined other Academicians in conveying the Academy's sympathy to the royal family after the death of the Dauphin (Registres, II, 593). On 25 August 1746, Voltaire participated in the annual celebration of the feast of Saint-Louis by reading an ode entitled *La Félicité des Temps ou l'Eloge de la France* (Registres, II, 594). The poem had been previously chosen by Voltaire's fellow Academicians. It is a rather flat and insincere piece of rhetoric which shows us Voltaire in the unbecoming role of the courtier. It contains the following description of France and its people:

> Vous verrez un peuple paisible,
> Généreux, aimable, invincible;
> Un prince au lieu de cent tyrans;
> Le joug porté sans esclavage;
> Et la concorde heureuse et sage
> Du roi, des peuples et des grands.
> (Moland, VIII, 458)

Following this special occasion, Voltaire's attendance fell drastically. He came to only one more meeting that year, to be present at the election of Charles Duclos on 22 September. Voltaire had a debt to repay to Duclos, who had courteously stepped aside at the time of Voltaire's election, and to whom Voltaire had preferred the abbé de La Ville when the next vacancy had occurred.[8] He was again present on 26 January 1747, when Duclos was received into the Academy and on 13 April 1747, when Academicians were received in audience

---

[8] The abbé de La Ville was received into the Academy on 15 September 1746. Voltaire's seeming ingratitude can be explained by the fact that La Ville's candidacy was sponsored by d'Argenson, who had also been instrumental in Voltaire's successful election. Thus, although Duclos was unquestionably superior to La Ville in the field of letters, Voltaire supported the latter because he was repaying a debt to his long-time protector, d'Argenson.

by the King, who accepted "les compliments de l'Académie française sur la mort de la reine de Pologne" (Registres, II, 608).[9] For 2 October 1747, we read the following entry in the Registers of the Academy: "Le sort a fait aujourd'hui M. de Voltaire Directeur de l'Académie, et M. l'Evêque de Mirepoix, Chancelier" (Registres, II, 617).[10] Voltaire was hardly more assiduous in his new function and presided over two meetings during his term of office, on 5 and 7 October 1747. He did not attend another meeting until almost two years later, on 7 June 1749, when the Maréchal de Belle-Isle was elected to the Academy. Soon afterwards Voltaire left his beloved Paris, not to return to it for a period of almost thirty years, and we have to wait until 1778 to see his name appear again on the list of the attending members.

Although Voltaire was absent from the Academy for the entire length of those twenty nine years, he took an active part in its life and followed with great interest its elections for a good portion of that time. It appears, however, that the years extending from the time of his election to approximately 1760 saw a gradual increase in Voltaire's indifference. Voltaire's poor attendance record during the years 1747, 1748 and 1749 can be partly explained by his sojourns at Cirey and at the court of Stanislas. Nevertheless, his absence from the Academy's meetings while he was in Paris is so obtrusive that it has led most historians to conclude that Voltaire lost all interest in the Academy once he had conquered it. The reasons put forth are various. They include harsh statements such as the following: "Il gardait rancune à l'Académie... Voltaire voulait donc, son discours de réception une fois prononcé, ou ne parler jamais à l'Académie, ou même n'y paraître jamais. Ainsi fit-il. Sa rancune dura plus de trente ans."[11] Other pronouncements are more perceptive: "Voltaire neither influenced the Academy as he had hoped, nor received from it the support he had expected. It is therefore no matter for surprise if, before his departure for Prussia, he showed complete indifference towards its

---

[9] "La reine de Pologne" refers to the King's mother-in-law, Catherine Opalinska, the wife of Stanislas Leszgzynski.

[10] The Academy had three officers, a director, a chancelor and a secretary. The former two were drawn by lot every two months; the secretary was elected for life.

[11] Charles Nisard, *Les Ennemis de Voltaire* (Paris: Amyot, 1853), p. 196.

activities." [12] Very often reasons are not given at all. They are nevertheless of the utmost importance if we are to understand the various attitudes Voltaire adopted vis à vis the Academy in the years following his election and if we are to appreciate the motives that governed these attitudes. The first step in this investigation will be to arrive at a clear concept of the significance the title of Academician held for Voltaire. It is necessary, therefore, to examine the reasons that gave Voltaire the will and the energy to pursue relentlessly academic honors for fifteen long years.

The first and most obvious motive, which occurred to Voltaire's contemporaries, as it comes to the mind of the student of Voltaire's life and works, is a very human and understandable one. Voltaire wanted the title for the glory it would bring him. It represented an appropriate crowning of his brilliant literary career, adding significantly to the prestige his name enjoyed in France and in all Europe. It would be, at the same time, a concrete sign of recognition, synonymous with newly gained favor in the eyes of the most eminent personalities of the kingdom, above all, in the eyes of the King himself. Voltaire never explicitly admitted the scope of his ambition. His claims were, on the contrary, extremely modest: on one occasion he stated, as we have seen, that a seat in the Academy was to him nothing but "un agrément frivole, la seule récompense que je demandais après trente années de travail" (Best. 2562, to d'Argental, 1 April 1743). Understatement was always one of Voltaire's favorite stylistic techniques.

Vanity was not, however, his only motive. Ever since his traumatic experience with the chevalier de Rohan, Voltaire had come to realize the precariousness of his situation as a man of letters. He had, consequently, striven to gain all the protection he could gather. Protection came, generally speaking, in two forms: in the guise of a personal relationship with a member of the high nobility, and in the form of an honorary title which placed the holder of the title under the tutelage of some recognized power, preferably the King himself. A place in the Academy offered one such form of security, and Voltaire very clearly thought of the Academy in those terms. In 1743 he explained to d'Argental: "La place, comme vous savez, est peu ou

---

[12] Conlon, p. 231.

rien, mais elle est beaucoup par les circonstances où je me trouve. La tranquillité de ma vie en dépend" (Best. 2541). He was even more explicit a few years later, when he reminisced about the difficulties and persecutions he had encountered in the years preceding his successful candidature of 1746: "Je songeai alors à me faire une espèce de rempart des académies contre les persécutions qu'un homme qui a écrit avec liberté doit toujours craindre en France" (Best. 3635, to Richelieu, 31 August 1750). Thus, even though the *Académie française* was by far the most important, it was not the only learned society to interest Voltaire. He did not succeed in gaining admittance to the *Académie des sciences* and to the *Académie des belles-lettres*,[13] but by the summer of 1746, he was a member of eighteen Academies. Seven of them were in France and included the Academies of Angers, Bordeaux, La Rochelle, Marseilles, Montpellier, Lyons and, of course, the *Académie française*; two in England, the Royal Society of London and of Edinburgh; in Italy there were seven, the Instituto di Bologna, the Arcadia, Crusca, Apatisti, Botanica of Florence, Etrusca of Cortona, Intronati; and finally the Academies of Prussia and of Saint Petersburg.[14]

The *Académie française* stood out so far above all the others because it undeniably was the most prestigious academic institution in Europe, and it seemed to offer by far the best protection, since it functioned under the aegis of the King of France. For Voltaire there existed yet a third reason why he had wanted so very much to become its member. A closer scrutiny of statements issued by Voltaire in reference to the Academy during the years preceding his election now becomes necessary.

At first glance Voltaire's remarks about the Academy present themselves as a confusing series of contradictions, a mixture of negative and positive comments. After careful analysis, however, a certain pattern emerges. The statements expressing Voltaire's criticisms, first of all, seem to have been dictated for the most part by feelings of resentment and vexation that grew from each unsuccessful candidature. This contention is supported by the fact that very often Voltaire's derogatory statements about the Academy followed closely each of

---

[13] Voltaire blamed d'Argenson's reluctance to support him for these failures (Best. 3635).
[14] Conlon, pp. 231-255.

his rejections. In addition, the content and tone of these passages do indicate "an element of sour grapes" (Best. IV, 193, note 14) in Voltaire's mood. In 1731, for example, Voltaire referred to the chair he so coveted as a "place méprisée par les gens qui pensent, respectée encore par la populace, et toujours courue par ceux qui n'ont que de la vanité" (Best. 435, to Formont, 25 December 1731). In 1733, after Voltaire had met with his second refusal, he mentioned "ce style efféminé, plein d'afféterie et vide de choses dont les frivoles auteurs de notre Académie française ont énervé notre langue" (Best. 632, to Jacob Vernet, 14 September 1733). In 1736, upon learning that Desfontaines was about to be imprisoned for having ridiculed the Academy, he found that the latter was "puni de ses crimes pour avoir fait une bonne action" (Best. 962, to Thiériot, 25 January 1736). Finally, in 1743, after being rejected for the last time, he wrote: "Une place à table à côté de mon cher Cideville vaut mieux qu'une place à l'académie. Ce n'est pas beaucoup dire. Je solliciteray toujours la première place et jamais la seconde" (Best. 2560, to Cideville, 23 March 1743).

On the other hand, we have two texts where a more serious and impartial Voltaire speaks at length of the Academy and its role. They are the chapter of the *Lettres philosophiques* entitled "Sur les Académies" and the so-called *Lettre sur les inconvénients attachés à la littérature*.[15] These works seem to have recorded a more permanent attitude on Voltaire's part, a deeper and more basic conviction, since they were written for publication and not on the spur of the moment, as were his letters. It is also to be noted that when the texts reappeared with additions or changes in later editions of Voltaire's works, their intent was never altered significantly, which leads us to believe that the author's outlook remained basically the same. These texts are generally known for the more derogatory remarks already quoted in Chapter I,[16] and other passages are rarely if ever cited. A distorted impression of Voltaire's intent has often been created, for the author's main purpose was not to mock and to ridicule the Academy, but to offer constructive criticisms and suggestions. The abuses he was attacking were real, and as we have seen, were deplored by a number of

---

[15] Besterman places its writing at some time between 1735 and 1742 (Best. Appendix 13, II, 420).
[16] See above, pp. 22-23.

his contemporaries as well. Voltaire found, first of all, that many of the Immortals were unworthy of their title: "On se plaint que la moitié des académiciens soit composée de seigneurs qui n'assistent jamais aux assemblées, et que dans l'autre moitié il se trouve à peine huit ou neuf gens de lettres qui soient assidus" (Best. II, 423). Secondly, Voltaire maintained that those who attended the Academy's meetings were engaged in the rather sterile task of turning out "des énormes recueils de vers médiocres, de compliments, de harangues" (Best. II, 423) and were neither doing a service to the Institution nor promoting the world of letters in France. Voltaire did not condemn the Academy itself for its shortcomings but excused it with Cicero's words "vitium est temporis potius quam hominis" and blamed tradition for keeping the Academy in its stagnant condition (Moland, XXII, 185).

At the same time, he had some definite thoughts on the role of the Academy, and not content with criticizing and condemning, Voltaire put forward recommendations intended to give the Academy new significance and renewed prestige. The *Lettre sur les Académies* contains an outline of his program:

> Pour l'Académie française, quel service ne rendrait-elle pas aux lettres, à la langue, et à la nation, si au lieu de faire imprimer tous les ans des compliments, elle faisait imprimer les bons ouvrages du siècle de Louis XIV, épurés de toutes les fautes de langage qui s'y sont glissées? Corneille et Molière en sont pleins, La Fontaine en fourmille: celles qu'on ne pourrait pas corriger seraient au moins marquées. L'Europe qui lit ces auteurs apprendrait par eux notre langue avec sûreté, sa pureté serait à jamais fixée; les bons livres français imprimés avec ce soin aux dépens du roi seraient un des plus glorieux monuments de la nation. (Moland, XXII, 186)

In the *Lettre sur les inconvénients attachés à la littérature* he made a similar proposal and stated: "Il est très certain que l'Académie française pourrait servir à fixer le goût de la nation" (Best. II, 423).

While outlining the course to follow, Voltaire was indicating indirectly that he would be the right person to help the Academy on this new path. That he was sincere in his designs became apparent on the day of his inauguration. His speech succeeded on two counts: it broke the traditional pattern of the empty inaugural rhetoric, and it reminded his fellow Academicians of their responsibility to advance the cause of French language and letters. The *Mémoires pour l'histoire des sciences et des beaux-arts* printed the following commentary of Voltaire's discourse:

> Quelques avis sur la décadence qui menace notre littérature se trouvent aussi placés très à propos dans ce discours. La qualité d'académicien est une sorte de magistrature par rapport au goût et à la langue. Les édiles de l'ancienne Rome ne durent pas conserver avec plus de soin l'ordre public, les censeurs ne durent pas plus veiller sur les mœurs des citoyens, que la première académie de ce royaume doit empêcher la barbarie de s'introduire dans nos manières de penser, de parler et d'écrire.[17]

Voltaire's message had been understood.

Yet, Voltaire made no further progress on his project. It was certainly not for lack of effort. In a letter to Frederick, Voltaire has left an account of some of the frustrations he encountered:

> Je roule aussi de petits projets dans ma teste pour donner plus de force et d'énergie à notre langue.... Votre majesté saura qu'à la dernière séance de notre académie où je me trouvay pour L'élection du maréchal de Belleîle, je proposay cette petite question: peut on dire, "un homme soudain dans ses transports, dans ses résolutions, dans sa colère"? comme on dit "un événement soudain"? Non, répondit on, car soudain n'apartient qu'aux choses inanimées.... J'eus beau faire, sire. Fontenelle, le cardinal de Rohan, mon amy l'ancien évêque de Mirepoix, jusqu'à l'abbé d'Olivet, tout fut contre moy. Je n'eus que deux suffrages pour mon soudain.... Si on laisse faire l'académie, elle apauvrira notre langue. (Best. 3453, 31 August 1749)

The projects Voltaire had conceived turned out very quickly to be mere illusions, and he soon realized that his fellow Academicians were not ready to be moved in any direction. He not only found it impossible to assert himself as a guide for the august body, but found it difficult to get along with his colleagues. They evidently resented Voltaire's rather presumptuous attitude and conflicts began to develop

---

[17] *Mémoires pour l'histoire des sciences et des beaux-arts*, June 1746, pp. 1343-1344.

soon after his election. Cideville found it necessary to reprove Voltaire in a letter written in September 1746:

> Vous ne ménagés point assés dans l'académie des gens, qui avoient déjà bien de la peine à vous passer votre supériorité. Vous l'avés trop fait sentir à plusieurs qui s'en sont plaints amèrement. N'avés vous point été bien fasché d'avoir reproché à un abé qui ne sait que lire qu'il ne savait pas lire? n'avés vous pas senti une pitié secrète en achevant à terre ce vieux lyrique?... Il faut estre doux avec ses inférieurs, et il n'est permis d'estre fier qu'avec ses égaux; et où sont les vostres? Laissés aux hommes leurs petites prétentions, on ne peut les leur arracher qu'avec la vie. (Best. 3131)

Voltaire apparently found it extremely difficult to be tolerant of the mediocrities that still occupied many of the chairs at the Academy. Indeed, the list of Academicians in 1746 is hardly more brilliant than that of 1731.[18] The Academy was still subject to the same criticisms that had been directed against it fifteen years earlier. The abbé d'Olivet, one of its most conscientious and respected members, confided his disenchantment to his friend Bouhier in 1745: "Parlons franchement; l'Académie ne peut rien sans un bon secrétaire; mais étant ce qu'elle est aujourd'hui, un bon secrétaire lui est inutile. Je n'y prends nulle part, Dieu merci, et il y a longtemps que je suis guéri d'un zèle dont vous avez pu voir encore quelque reste."[19] As late as 1750, some of the choices of the Academy were subjecting it to further ridicule. Collé was indignant following the election of the Comte de Bissy: "Le choix de l'Académie, dans cette occasion, lui a donné un ridicule affreux, et l'a fait tomber même dans une espèce d'avilissement. S'ils continuent à recevoir des Seigneurs de l'espèce de M. de Bissy, les gens de la Cour trouveront au-dessous d'eux d'y entrer; ils feront bientôt donner ces places à leurs secrétaires ou du moins à des *manans* qu'ils protégeront."[20] The pleasure Voltaire took in his success must have waned considerably as he became better acquainted with some of his colleagues.

Voltaire was further embittered by the fact that the atmosphere he encountered within the Academy was far from congenial. Obviously,

---

[18] A list of the members of the French Academy in 1746 is given in Appendix B, pp. 133-134.
[19] Pellisson and d'Olivet, II, 450.
[20] Charles Collé, *Journal et mémoires* (Paris: Didot, 1868), I, 314 and 315.

he had not expected every Academician to be his friend as soon as he became one of the Immortal Forty. Nevertheless he had imagined that he would find himself in a milieu not unlike that of a fraternity of cultured and literary men. A few days before his election he had written to Moncrif: "C'est peu de chose d'entrer dans une compagnie, il faut y être reçu comme on l'est chez ses amis, voilà ce qui rend une telle place infiniment désirable" (Best. 3060, 23 April 1746). Voltaire's statement, which at first appears to be mere epistolary rhetoric, takes on added significance when we see him develop further this theme of friendship in his inaugural speech. In it he speaks of the "charme que l'amitié répand sur les travaux des hommes consacrés aux lettres," points out that the Academy had been founded "dans le sein de l'amitié" and that "les vrais amateurs des arts sont amis." He expresses the hope that "la bienséance, l'union, la candeur, la saine critique si opposée à la satire" which governed the meetings of the founding members will continue to preside over assemblies of the present Academy (Moland, XXIII, 214-215). He was to find out that this was but another illusion which had deluded him.

To make Voltaire's disillusionment complete, yet a third disappointment awaited him. He was to discover that he was hardly more secure inside the Academy than he had been outside of it and that his position remained just as vulnerable. In 1748 he sought in vain the Academy's protection when a parody of *Sémiramis* was about to be performed at the court of Versailles. He wrote to d'Argental: "Mes anges, engagez m. l'abbé de Bernis à ne pas abandonner son confrère, à ne pas souffrir un opprobre qui avilit l'académie" (Best. 3299, 10 October 1748). The attacks of his enemies, as we have seen, became even fiercer the year of his election, and his title of Academician seemed to attract only more troubles instead of affording him the shelter he had expected. Voltaire's biographer, Condorcet, notes: "il croyait qu'il trouverait dans l'académie un appui contre la persécution; et c'était présumer trop du courage et de la justice de ses confrères" (Moland, I, 255). The discovery that membership in the Academy did not contribute noticeably to making his life more pleasant in France was probably one of the more important factors that led Voltaire to his decision to leave France in 1750.

Disappointed inside the Academy, Voltaire was experiencing vexations outside as well, as several incidents gravely impaired his position at the court. There was the madrigal he had written to flatter Mme de Pompadour, which greatly displeased the Queen instead; there was also the remark he made during a card game, accusing the aristocratic participants of cheating and "so ... came to an end his painful efforts to acquire favour at court" (Best. XV, XXII). Frederick II, in the meantime, was making Berlin sound more and more attractive in his letters and was constantly reminding Voltaire (as he had been doing for some ten years) of the injustices and persecutions the latter had to endure in France. When Mme Du Châtelet died on 10 September 1749, one of the strongest ties binding him to his country broke, and soon after he was on his way to Prussia. We are not surprised to find out that Louis XV did not lament Voltaire's departure. The marquis de Puisieulx informed the comte Tyrconnell: "Vous apprendrez que le roi de Prusse a fait demander Voltaire au roi. Sa majesté le lui a accordé. Elle a pensé que cette complaisance serait agréable à ce prince, et que si d'un côté elle laissait aller un académicien que quelqu'uns de ses ouvrages rendent célèbre elle n'avait d'ailleurs rien à regretter dans ce sacrifice" (Best. 3623, 22 August 1750). Voltaire's academic title had apparently failed to influence or change to any significant degree the King's attitude towards him.

Voltaire had not found it very easy to arrive at his decision to leave France. In the *Commentaire historique* he recalls that "Il était parti après avoir combattu pendant plus de six mois contre toute sa famille et contre tous ses amis" (Moland, I, 92). Yet, remembering all the unfavorable circumstances and unpleasant incidents that had troubled his existence in his own country, he found, for a time at least, that his choice had been the right one. He stated as much in several of his letters written to friends in the second half of 1750. He communicated to Richelieu: "Le roi de Prusse me traite aussi bien qu'on me traitait mal chez moi" (Best. 3635, 31 August 1750), and to d'Argental: "Ma foi, mon cher ange, j'ai fort bien fait de quitter ce beau pays là, et de jouir du repos auprès d'un héros, à l'abri de la canaille qui me persécutait, des graves pédants qui ne me défendaient pas, des dévots qui, tôt ou tard, m'auraient joué un mauvais tour, et de l'envie qui ne cesse de sucer le sang quand on n'en a plus" (Best. 3706, 28 November 1750).

Voltaire's choice of the expression "graves pédants" would seem to indicate a certain amount of resentment held against the Academy and leads us back to the principal consideration in this chapter, namely Voltaire's growing indifference toward the Company of Immortals. It seems clear that the statement "il a bien assez de songer à ses intérêts et à sa sûreté. ... La décadence de la compagnie le laisse en réalité fort indifférent" [21] does not reproduce very accurately Voltaire's attitude at the time of his election. It chooses to ignore the very real interest Voltaire had in the functioning of the Academy and the concern with which he regarded its role. It appears necessary at the present juncture to determine whether Voltaire still had this interest or concern when he left France, or if indeed "he showed complete indifference towards its activities." [22]

The first clue to Voltaire's sentiments regarding the Academy at that time is to be found in his correspondence with Frederick II. The King of Prussia quite frequently included derogatory remarks about the Academy in his letters to Voltaire, both before the latter's election and after. He obviously did this to add fuel to the resentment Voltaire naturally felt as a result of his frustrating experiences with the learned Society. Before 1746, Voltaire willingly responded in kind and readily composed his own diatribes such as the one, written in 1740, describing the members of the Academy as:

> Ces gens doctement ridicules,
> Parlant de rien, nourris de vent,
> Et qui pèsent si gravement
> Des mots, des points et des virgules.
>   (Best. 2071, 15 April 1740)

In 1749, however, Frederick's proddings elicited extremely mild responses and when the King wrote:

> Qui veut le suffrage et l'estime
> De ces quarante perroquets
> N'a qu'à savoir son catéchisme
> Au demeurant point de français.
>   (Best. 3415, 15 July 1749)

Voltaire answered with verses that seem to have been inspired principally by courtesy:

---

[21] Brunel, p. 45.
[22] Conlon, p. 231.

> J'ay reçu vos vers très plaisants
> Sur notre triste académie.
> Nos quarante sont fort savants,
> Des mots ils sentent l'énergie,
> Et de prose et de poésie
> Ils donnent des prix tous les ans.
> Ils font surtout des compliments
> Mais aucun n'a votre génie.
>
> (Best. 3440, 17 August 1749)

Furthermore, the criticism contained in these lines is only a fair evaluation of the Company at the time Voltaire wrote his letter and repeats the specific disapprobation he had already voiced upon several occasions. Voltaire's sentiments concerning the Academy had mellowed because upon his election his principal grudge had vanished. The resentment had given way to a newer and more complex attitude which emerges from Voltaire's general correspondence of the year 1749.

If we examine Voltaire's letters written during the period immediately preceding the death of Mme Du Châtelet we see that approximately every second one contains a reference to the Academy. Voltaire inquired about the election that took place in August 1749 and indicated his preferences by expressing support for his favorite candidates (Best. 3433, 3434, 3441, 3445, 3448, 3459). In addition, the insistence with which Voltaire used the term *confrère* in his letters when writing to a fellow Academician or when referring to a fellow member or a potential fellow member points to a certain amount of pride he took in his recently gained title (Best. 3433, 3434, 3440, 3441, 3443, 3459, for example). It appears also that he willingly continued to meet with a number of Academicians on an informal basis whenever he was in Paris. He wrote the following invitation to Destouches in February of 1750: "Venez donc, mon illustre ami, mardi à trois heures; vous trouverez quelques académiciens nos confrères" (Best. 3536). The tone of these letters tends to indicate that a feeling of solidarity rather than indifference characterized Voltaire's attitude at the time and his correspondence in general shows that, although he was not directly participating in the Academy's functions, he was well aware of its activities.

There were two occasions when he had an indirect part to play in these activities. In the early part of 1749, at the request of Richelieu, Voltaire wrote a short discourse with which the maréchal intended to compliment the King on the recently concluded peace treaty of Aix-la-Chapelle. On 21 February, shortly before the whole Academy was to be received by the King, Richelieu discovered that his speech had somehow been made public. We do not know for certain if the *maréchal* did give the speech as planned or if he improvised his own. One thing is sure, Richelieu was irritated. As a result, he failed to present to the King a panegyric in five languages that Voltaire had issued upon the occasion, and thus took revenge for the supposed treachery of his friend. It was soon discovered that the poet had not been responsible for divulging the discourse; nevertheless, the incident had not served Voltaire in his renewed efforts to court Louis XV.[23] A few months later, Voltaire consented to write a sermon for a certain abbé d'Arty, who had been chosen to deliver one to the Academicians assembled for the St. Louis-Day Mass that year. Having added an "Ave-Maria" and an "Ainsi soit-il," the abbé d'Arty delivered the sermon with great success, published it in his own name, and was subsequently recompensed with a bishopric for his accomplishment.[24]

Voltaire never divorced himself from the Academy, simply because the original reasons which had motivated his candidacies were still valid. First, in spite of the frustrations he had encountered, he still saw the Academy as a protector. In a letter written to Mme Denis in 1754 we read: "J'ai envoyé à l'Académie française et à celle des Inscriptions les désaveux authentiques de la malheureuse édition faite à la Haye" (Best. 4973, 5 January 1754). In 1755, when spurious editions of some of his works were being circulated in France, he addressed himself to the Company demanding its support in an eloquent letter which ended with the following passage: "C'est à vous,

---

[23] The anecdote is related by Longchamp in his *Mémoires*; see Longchamp et Wagnière, *Mémoires sur Voltaire* (Paris: Aimé André, 1826), II, 180-183. *The Compliment Fait au Roi, sur la Paix conclue avec la Reine de Hongrie et de Bohème, Impératrice, et le Roi de la Grande-Bretagne, par M. le Maréchal Duc de Richelieu, Directeur* was published in 1753 in a *Recueil* of the Academy's discourses, which would lead us to believe, contrary to Longchamp's assertion, that Richelieu did deliver the speech after all.

[24] Longchamp et Wagnière, II, 236-245. See also Best. vol. XVII, Appendix 51. The memory of Saint-Louis was celebrated on 25 August. It was a most solemn occasion for the Academy; its members attended Mass in the morning, and in the afternoon held a meeting open to the public, in which the annual prizes for poetry and eloquence were presented.

messieurs, et aux académies formées sur votre modèle, dont j'ai l'honneur d'être associé, que je dois m'adresser. Lorsque des hommes, comme vous, élèvent leurs voix pour réprouver tous ces ouvrages que l'ignorance et l'avidité débitent, le public que vous éclairez est bientôt désabusé" (Best. 5916, 14 November 1755). He then took pains to have his letter circulated and published in a number of newspapers in France, Switzerland and Germany. He received a favorable answer from Duclos, the Secretary of the Academy (Best. 5928, 20 November), and was apparently gratified with the Academy's reaction, for he thanked the Company a month later (Best. 5976, 21 December). This exchange of courtesies clearly indicates that the old aggravations had been forgotten and announces already a new era in the relationship between the philosophe and the Society.

Secondly, Voltaire's respect for the Academy as a defender of purity and taste in linguistic and literary matters had been preserved despite his initial disappointing contact with the membership. This is evidenced by some of his letters to Frederick written at the time he was preparing to leave France. Whenever Voltaire mentions a grammatical or literary point, he brings up the subject of the Academy. The reference to the Company is sometimes serious, sometimes playful, but it shows that in Voltaire's mind, the name of the Academy was readily associated with linguistic matters. A few years later, Voltaire clearly expressed his confidence in the role of the Academy in a letter to his former teacher d'Olivet, after the latter had sent him the *Opuscules sur la langue française*. On receiving d'Olivet's book, he found that "ce petit livre très instructif prouve que l'Académie est plus utile qu'on ne pense, et il fait voir en même temps combien vous êtes utile à l'Académie" (Best. 5100, 26 March 1754). This particular aspect of Voltaire's attitude toward the Academy is also reflected in some of the works he wrote or edited during his first years as Academician. While discussing French literature of the first half of the seventeenth century in the *Siècle de Louis XIV*, he credited the Academy and one of its founding members with an important historical role: "La langue commençait à s'épurer et à prendre une forme constante. On en était redevable à l'Académie française, et surtout à Vaugelas" (Moland, XIV, 157). Voltaire stressed also the importance of the Academy in the introduction of the same work by stating that "le siècle que j'appelle de Louis XIV ... commence à peu près à l'établissement de l'Académie française" (Moland, XIV, 157).

In 1748 and in 1752 Voltaire modified the "Lettre sur les Académies" with two additions which further clarify his views on the significance of the Academy. The newly added statements emphasized mainly the practical value of the Institution. Thus, in 1748, he wrote that "les grands hommes se sont tous formés ou avant les Académies ou indépendamment d'elles." After giving illustrations to substantiate this statement, he concluded that an Academy's principal function was to "entretenir le feu que les grands génies ont allumé" (Moland, XXII, 183). One way to do this, as he had already pointed out, was to publish critical editions of the great works of literature, expurgated of what Voltaire considered impurities of language and of style. In 1752, Voltaire offered specific suggestions regarding the works of one of "les grands génies" that interested him in particular. He observed:

> Une chose assez singulière, c'est que Corneille, qui écrivait avec assez de pureté et beaucoup de noblesse les premières de ses bonnes tragédies, lorsque la langue commençait à se former, écrivit toutes les autres très incorrectement et d'un style très bas, dans le temps que Racine donnait à la langue française tant de pureté, de vraie noblesse et de grâces, dans le temps que Despréaux la fixait par l'exactitude la plus correcte, par la précision, la force et l'harmonie. (Moland, XXII, 187).

It is to be noted that the passage already contains the general idea that was to govern Voltaire's *Commentaire sur Corneille,* undertaken eight years later, under the auspices of the Academy.

The subject offered him also the occasion to air personal grudges concerning the existing state of literature in France: "Ce qui est encore plus étrange, c'est que de notre temps même nous avons eu des pièces de théâtre, des ouvrages de prose et de poésie, composés par des académiciens qui ont négligé leur langue, au point qu'on ne trouve pas chez eux dix vers ou dix lignes de suite sans quelque barbarisme." Voltaire observed that such works are sometimes well received by the public and reissued the warning against literary decadence he had already voiced in his inaugural speech: "Deux ou trois succès pareils suffiraient pour corrompre la langue sans retour et pour la faire retomber dans son ancienne barbarie, dont les soins assidus de tant de grands hommes l'ont tirée" (Moland, XXII, 187). Lanson has pointed out [25] that this addition was aimed principally at Crébillon, whose *Catalina* was staged in 1748 and was well received by the Court. If Voltaire did have a specific author in mind when writing these lines, the theme of literary decadence appears with such frequency under his pen that we cannot discount a more general intent. Crébillon's example may have been suggested by Voltaire only as a "case in point" illustration to give more weight to the warning.

While Voltaire was reminding his fellow Academicians of their duty to French language and literature, he himself was caught in events that forced him to neglect his Academic duties for the time being. He was to remain outside of France for the major portion of the decade stretching from 1750 to 1760. These were very troubled and traumatic years in his life, and in general he did not maintain a very close contact with the Academy; he occasionally followed with interest some of the elections and in 1758 made arrangements to have his portrait sent to the Academy. These are the years which saw a profound transformation take place in him and which truly mark the beginning of the "Age of Voltaire," for it is around this time that "Voltaire became utterly committed to the fight for the Enlightenment." [26]

In the meantime, changes had been taking place inside the French Academy as well. New members were bringing fresh ideas to the Company, and with the election of d'Alembert in 1754, the Academy slowly began veering away from its conventional ways. It was soon thereafter that Voltaire and the Academy rediscovered each other, and the ties that existed already between the Society and its most illustrious member were to be considerably strengthened.

---

[25] Voltaire, *Lettres philosophiques*, ed. Gustave Lanson, Second ed. (Paris: Hachette, 1915-1917), II, 183.

[26] Theodore Besterman, *Voltaire* (New York: Harcourt, Brace and World, 1969), p. 360.

CHAPTER III

THE ACADEMIC BATTLEGROUND

The years during which Voltaire showed little active interest in the Academy form one of the most trying and troubled periods of his life. Aggravated in the beginning by a severe case of depression [1] and failing health, the chain of events that started with Mme Du Châtelet's death left a profound mark upon Voltaire's thought. The Prussian episode, the Seven Years' War and the Lisbon earthquake were some of the more telling experiences that left Voltaire "a man obsessed, tormented by the spectacle of a humanity that suffered and was resigned to suffering" [2] and by the time he had settled at Ferney, he was ready to lead the crusade for Enlightenment. It is in this spirit that he had started collaborating with the Encyclopedists, and although most of the articles he contributed were comparatively innocuous, the experience had given him new insights: "The encyclopedic cause had imbued him with a sense of mission and had opened before him the vision of his role as leader and defender of the Philosophes." [3] As the decade of the fifties drew to a close, the conflicts between the philosophes and the authorities became considerably sharper and a returning motif in Voltaire's correspondence towards this time is a call for unity in the ranks of the brothers: "Voilà le temps où tous les philosophes devraient se réunir" (Best. 6937, Voltaire to the comte de

---

[1] René Pomeau calls it "la grande crise dépressive qui termine la période de Cirey." René Pomeau, *La Religion de Voltaire* (Paris: Nizet, 1956), p. 234.
[2] Besterman, *Voltaire*, p. 358.
[3] John N. Pappas, *Voltaire and d'Alembert* (Bloomington: Indiana University Press, 1962), p. 12.

Tressan, 13 February, 1758). Voltaire was prepared to lead the struggle and to fight on all fronts in order to further the cause of the Enlightenment.[4] One of the battlegrounds was to be the *Académie française*.

There is nothing to indicate that Voltaire had ever intended before 1760 to bring the struggle to the Academy. The Institution as such was in no way endangering the cause of the philosophes, on the contrary, there were signs pointing to a gradually changing attitude within the Company. Already in 1750 the *Nouvelles ecclésiastiques* had noted with alarm that: "Il se glisse dans les Académies un esprit qui doit allarmer ceux qui ont de la religion."[5] The elections of Duclos in 1746 and of d'Alembert in 1754 were among the events that contributed most to the transformation that was to take place in the Academy. The two men held widely divergent views on the role of the Institution. Nevertheless, they were both responsible for giving the Academy renewed importance and prestige in the second half of the eighteenth century. Since the single most important function inside the Academy was that of the *secrétaire perpétuel*, the influence exerted by the two men was especially great during the time they each held that office; Duclos served as secretary from 1755 to 1772 and l'Alembert from 1772 to 1783.

In 1760 the Academy was still far from the importance and the prestige it was to enjoy later, when it had truly become a bastion of the philosophes.[6] Historians of the Academy have often been inexact in evaluating the Institution in this respect. To say, for example, that with the election of Voltaire in 1746 "c'est le règne de la Philosophie qui commence"[7] is to commit a serious anachronism by antedating the beginning of the reign by approximately twenty years. The fact is that d'Alembert was the only true philosophe attending the Academy's meetings in 1760. Duclos, the Academy's secretary, was to become a valuable ally of the philosophes, but in general he was

---

[4] John Pappas points out that Voltaire's *Ode sur la mort de la markgrave de Bareith* written in 1759 "is in fact a public announcement that henceforth, those who attack the encyclopedists must answer to Voltaire." *The Journal de Trévoux*, p. 119.

[5] *Les Nouvelles Ecclésiastiques,* 13 février 1750, p. 26.

[6] The list of the members of the French Academy in 1760, at the time of Pompignan's reception, is found in Appendix C, pp. 135-136.

[7] Gassier, p. 97.

"much more concerned with restoring to the Academy its proper literary function than with making it a vehicle for the propagation of free-thinking ideas." [8] Duclos's own statement in his *Histoire de l'Académie françoise* is a good example of his rather conservative outlook: "Rien ne prouve mieux la sagesse d'un établissement que le peu de changement qu'il éprouve durant une longue suite d'années." [9] Voltaire was well aware of Duclos's moderate stance. He was to remark in 1764: "Je crois que ce secrétaire ne sera jamais l'ennemi de la philosophie; mais je ne crois pas qu'il veuille se compromettre pour elle" (Best. 11205, Voltaire to Damilaville, 9 August 1764). A few other Academicians were doubtless receptive to the ideas of Enlightenment but had none of the militancy exhibited by d'Alembert.

The situation as it existed in the Academy in the beginning of 1760 was obviously not too propitious to the project d'Alembert had recently conceived: to make the Institution a stronghold of the philosophe party. It appears that d'Alembert decided upon this particular course of action soon after his resignation as co-editor of the *Encyclopédie* in 1757. Thereafter he considered the Academy as a suitable substitute for the propagation of the *esprit philosophique* and "the meaning of his academician's career must be constantly interpreted within this wider context of 'philosophical' strategy." [10] To carry out this strategy his principal ally was to be Voltaire. The two philosophes had become acquainted while working on the *Encyclopédie* and the friendship and respect they had for each other were to be preserved, in spite of minor clashes on matters of policy and tactics, until Voltaire's death. [11] In addition to the affinity in personality traits, the two men felt they had a need for each other in their struggle for Enlightenment. For d'Alembert, Voltaire was to be the defender of the *frères*, able to express himself freely from his refuge in Ferney. D'Alembert, in turn, was to provide a necessary link with Paris and the Academy and was to keep him informed on the latest developments in the capital and on the progress made my their cause. In addition, d'Alembert saw it his role to add prestige to the philosophe party by

---

[8] Ronald Grimsley, *Jean d'Alembert* (Oxford: Clarendon Press, 1963), p. 78.

[9] Charles Duclos, *Œuvres Complètes* (Paris: Belin, 1821), I, 569.

[10] Grimsley, p. 106.

[11] For a complete study of this relationship, see Pappas, *Voltaire and d'Alembert*.

getting members of the sect elected to the Academy: "The master was to defend the party with his pen, while his disciple recruited new members and increased their prestige." [12] We see from the Voltaire-d'Alembert correspondence that this arrangement was already taking shape before 1760. At the time the Encyclopedists were being persecuted Voltaire wrote: "Je n'en sais rien; je vois tout de trop loin. Mettez moi au fait, je vous en prie" (Best. 6923, 5 February 1758). D'Alembert, on the other hand, encouraged his friend not to spare their enemies: "Mon cher ami, frappez fort; vous êtes en place marchande pour cela" (Best. 7578, 13 May 1759). Soon afterwards, events provided Voltaire with an excellent opportunity to play his role of defender of the philosophic sect: the "brothers" had been attacked within the Academy itself.

We have seen that neither d'Alembert nor Voltaire had any intention of creating an open conflict between the faction of the *dévots* and the philosophes inside the Academy. They were both merely interested in consolidating the position of their party within the Company. Thus in 1758 Voltaire had expressed his concern about the friction that existed between d'Alembert and Duclos: "Est ce là le temps où les ennemis de la superstition devraient se brouiller?" (Best. 6936, to d'Alembert, 13 February 1758). Suddenly, Voltaire and d'Alembert found themselves on the defensive following the unexpected attack Le Franc de Pompignan made on the day he was received into the Academy. Le Franc de Pompignan, who had been elected to the chair of Maupertuis, gave his inaugural speech on 10 March 1760. The central theme of his discourse was a vehement attack against the new and rapidly spreading "philosophical" spirit. Pompignan's principal motive was probably a desire to please the royal family, for he had hopes of becoming the governor of the royal children. [13] Luckily for the philosophes, the discourse was delivered in such a haughty and pompous manner that it was made to be ridiculed. In writing an account of the speech, Grimm noted that "il s'est attaché principalement à nous laisser soupçonner que lui, récipiendaire, était un très-grand homme." [14] Collé was also critical: "Ce sermon ne me paroît pas avoir réussi du tout ... les dévots mêmes ne lui savent pas grand gré de

---

[12] *Ibid.*, p. 41.
[13] Desnoiresterres, V, 419.
[14] Grimm, IV, 236.

sa malignité chrétienne ou non chrétienne." The speech was mainly criticized for its pretentiousness. Thus, Pompignan had not even found it necessary to give the customary thanks to the Academy but had shocked many of the Academicians by using the phrase "appelé par vos suffrages." [15] The philosophes had even more reason to be shocked, for the accusation brought against them placed them in a dangerous situation. Pompignan's discourse contained clear allusions to four of the Academicians: Duclos, Buffon, d'Alembert and Voltaire, and the author denounced *la philosophie* for undermining the throne and the altar. The accusation was extremely serious: "Que Pompignan eût dénoncé la philosophie comme 'sapant l'autel,' cela était admissible, mais qu'il eût ajouté: 'et le trône,' cela faisait bondir les encyclopédistes, dont tous les actes démentaient cette affirmation." [16] At a time when both Voltaire and d'Alembert were striving to gain support for their cause, these allegations could have seriously impaired their enterprise. It was necessary to react swiftly and effectively. An anonymous pamphlet entitled *les Quand* soon began circulating. It was composed of several paragraphs each beginning with *Quand* and ended with the following admonition: "Quand on est admis dans un corps respectable, il faut dans sa harangue, cacher sous les voiles de la modestie l'insolent orgueil qui est le partage des têtes chaudes et des talents médiocres" (Moland, XXIV, 113). When d'Alembert received a copy of the booklet sent to him from Geneva, he wrote to the suspected author of the satire: "Quand on a le bonheur d'être dans un pays libre, mon cher et grand Philosophe, on est bien heureux; car on peut écrire librement pour la défense des Philosophes, contre les invectives de ceux qui ne le sont pas" (Best. 8114, 14 April 1760). The abbé Morellet followed up with the *si* and the *pourquoi*, then Voltaire came back with the *qui*, the *quoi*, the *oui*, the *non*, the *car*, the *ah! ah!*, the satirical poems *le Pauvre Diable*, *le Russe à Paris* and *la Vanité*. The story of Pompignan's misfortunes is too well known to be told here. [17] Suffice it to say that Pompignan's discomfiture was so complete that he never dared to reappear in the Academy. It was apparently a wise decision, for on 30 June 1760 d'Argental informed Voltaire: "S'il

---

[15] Collé, II, 221.

[16] Mario Roustan, *Les Philosophes et la société française au XVIIIe siècle* (Lyon: A. Rey, 1906), p. 58.

[17] For a complete account of these events, see for example Desnoiresterres, vol. V, chapter X; also Brunel pp. 73-90.

paroit à l'Académie le parti est pris de ne point luy parler" (Best. 8270).

The philosophes had won a great moral victory, thanks principally to the unrelenting harassment inflicted by Voltaire's pen. The patriarch of Ferney had shown such impetuosity because he had, first of all, personally been offended by Pompignan's allegations. On 20 June 1760 he complained to Duclos: "Il ne fallait pas outrager un vieillard retiré du monde" (Best. 8248). He explained to Mme Du Deffand on 14 July 1760 that Pompignan and his associates had had the following intentions: "Leur projet était d'armer le gouvernement contre tous ceux qu'ils accusent d'être philosophes, de me faire exclure de l'académie... et de purifier ainsi le sanctuaire profané" (Best. 8312).[18] Voltaire was probably more concerned, however, about Pompignan's attempt to discredit the philosophes in general; the danger for them had been very real. Fréron's newssheet quoted the following commentary, which the King had made on the subject of Pompignan's discourse: "C'est un excellent ouvrage, selon moi, peu fait, au reste, pour être applaudi par les impies et les esprits forts."[19] Voltaire found it necessary to explain his reasons for attacking Pompignan upon a number of occasions to his friends, and as late as September 1763 we see him writing to Helvétius: "Si on n'avait pas confondu ce malheureux, l'usage d'insulter les philosophes dans les discours de réception à l'académie, aurait passé en loy. Si on n'avait pas rendu nos persécuteurs ridicules, ils n'auraient pas mis de bornes à leur insolence" (Best. 10595).

The philosophes had weathered quite well this unexpected assault and remained victorious on the battlefield, having fortified their position with one precious advantage: Pompignan's fate loomed large enough to discourage any imitators. The pretense of a peaceful coexistence in the Academy had been shattered meanwhile, and the philosophes had to consolidate their gains by further victories for fear of losing the influence they already possessed. These were probably some of the considerations that had suggested a new project to Voltaire: he had become obsessed with getting Diderot elected to the

---

[18] Favart also mentions Pompignan's intention to get Voltaire expelled from the Academy. Charles S. Favart, *Mémoires et correspondance littéraires, dramatiques et anecdotiques* (Paris: Collin, 1808), I, 46.

[19] *L'Année littéraire*, 30 March 1760, II, 277.

Academy. He presented his arguments to d'Alembert on 9 July: "En un mot il faut mettre Diderot à l'académie. C'est la plus belle vengeance qu'on puisse tirer de la pièce contre les philosophes. L'académie est indignée contre le Franc de Pompignan. Elle luy donnera avec grand plaisir ce souflet à tour de bras" (Best. 8296) [20] For several months Voltaire relentlessly assailed his friends with similar explanations, namely, that Diderot's election would be a fitting revenge for the defamatory attacks of Pompignan and Palissot. He even promised to come to Paris to cast his vote (Best. 8298 and 8336) and outlined a course of action that is very reminiscent of his own tactics used some fifteen years earlier to gain entrance into the Citadel of the Immortals. He was very confident of the outcome and thought that Diderot could easily get a majority of the votes "si en allant voir les dévôts, il les persuade de sa religion" (Best. 8334, to Mme d'Epinay, 24 July 1760). Voltaire even addressed himself to one of the *dévots*, the abbé d'Olivet, arguing that: "Vous sçavez qu'il ne faut pas que l'académie soit un séminaire et qu'elle ne doit pas être la cour des pairs. Quelques ornements d'or à notre Lyre sont convenables: mais il faut que les cordes soient à boyeau, et qu'elles soient sonores" (Best. 8797, 22 January 1761). Voltaire was, of course, referring to Diderot's undeniable talents and recognized stature as a man of letters. In a similar vein, he had already pointed out to Duclos that Diderot could be extremely valuable to the Academy at a time when the Company had started to work on a new edition of the dictionary (Best. 8378). In order to encourage his friends, Voltaire also promised the backing of Mme de Pompadour and the minister Choiseul. In this respect, the election of Diderot would have added strength to a point of view held by Voltaire which d'Alembert could never accept: that the cause of the philosophes could be furthered by courting the *puissances*. [21]

Voltaires efforts brought no results. D'Argental had informed him as early as 22 July 1760 that circumstances were extremely unfavorable and suggested and alternative plan:

---

[20] "la pièce contre les philosophes" refers to Palissot's *Les Philosophes* which was being shown at that time.

[21] Pappas, *Voltaire and d'Alembert*, p. 24. On this subject, see also Raymond Naves, *Voltaire et l'Encyclopédie* (Paris: Les Editions des Presses modernes, 1938), pp. 79 and 80.

> J'ai fait quelques tentatives en faveur de Diderot conformément à votre projet et à vos intentions. On m'a répondu sans aigreur, sans amertume, mais de façon à ne laisser aucune espérance. Il faudrait peut être passer par l'échelon de l'académie des sciences. Il y a dans cette académie plus de philosophes et moins de prêtraille que dans l'académie françoise, par conséquent moins d'obstacles à vaincre. (Best. 8339)

D'Alembert also was reluctant to go along with Voltaire's plans because, he explained, "cela feroit une guerre civile," the King would never accept and the *dévots* would certainly triumph (Best. 8428, 2 September 1760). Finally, the candidate himself appeared unwilling to seek Academic honors. He was clearly annoyed at Voltaire's persistent campaigning and wrote to Sophie Volland: "A propos de Voltaire, il se plaint à Grimm très amèrement de mon silence: il dit qu'il est au moins de la politesse de remercier son avocat. Et qui diable l'a prié de plaider ma cause?" [22] Diderot's testiness was caused in part by his distrust of Voltaire, who continued courting *les puissances* and showed extreme moderation in dealing with Palissot. [23] It is possible, in addition, that his unconcern for the Academy was not feigned; he occasionally expressed it in later years. Thus in April 1764 Diderot was to refer to the institution as "l'Académie française, dont je ne suis, ni ne serai jamais." [24] The following passage of Grimm's *Correspondance,* written in 1768, is also illustrative of Diderot's subsequent attitude: "Un Anglais causant dernièrement avec M. Diderot lui disait: 'Je ne sais comment vous avez fait en France pour fixer votre langue depuis plus de cent ans et la rendre pour ainsi dire immuable, tandis que la notre varie sans cesse et n'a point de règle constante. — C'est monsieur, lui répondit le philosophe, que vous n'avez pas comme nous quarante oies qui gardent le Capitole'." [25]

Diderot's election to the Academy was not a simple obsession for Voltaire. It is clear that "his election would have been a tremendous victory for philosophy." [26] Voltaire, as we have seen, never tired of

---

[22] Diderot, *Correspondance,* ed. Georges Roth (Paris: Editions de Minuit, 1955-1966), III, 247.
[23] Naves, *Voltaire et l'Encyclopédie,* p. 80. Also, Arthur M. Wilson, *Diderot* (New York: Oxford Univ. Press, 1972), p. 400.
[24] Diderot, IV, 293.
[25] Grimm, VIII, 167.
[26] Norman Lewis Torrey, "Voltaire's Reaction to Diderot," *PMLA,* L (1935), 1114.

repeating this argument to his friends. In addition, the patriarch of Ferney was apparently motivated by a concern for Diderot's safety and well being, for on 25 February 1761 he wrote to Damilaville: "Je crois qu'il faut tout tenter pour mettre m. Diderot de l'académie; c'est toujours une espèce de rempart contre les fanatiques et les fripons" (Best. 8877). Finally Voltaire had to abandon his plans. He did so with great reluctance, and occasionally returned to the idea after everyone else had abandoned it, even while he was promoting other candidates. In 1761, for example, he wrote to Marmontel: "J'espérais vous avoir pour confrère et qu'ensuite vous ouvririez la porte à mr Diderot" (Best. 8782).

Although Voltaire's designs to get Diderot elected have sometimes been characterized as unrealistic and foolish, it is understandable that, from his vantage point at Ferney, the obstacles confronting Diderot did not appear more forbidding than the ones he himself had faced fifteen years earlier. D'Alembert also had been elected a few years before, in spite of stiff opposition. Finally, the election of the two *encyclopédistes*, La Condamine and Watelet, in 1760, was certainly an encouraging sign. What Voltaire did not know, was that the Academies were officially closed to Diderot.[27] While the government was willing to accept some degree of philosophic influence in the Academy, there obviously were limits to its tolerance, even at this early stage of d'Alembert's campaign.

In spite of their early successes, the philosophes were still extremely weak inside the Academy. The following three candidates entering the Company in 1761, were all sponsored by the party of the *dévots*. Writing to Voltaire after the election of l'abbé Trublet, d'Alembert sounded bitter and pointed out that the philosophes could not always depend on their allies inside the Academy: "Remerciez, je vous prie, de la belle acquisition que nous venons de faire, votre ami d'Olivet, le petit duc de Nivernois, aussi chafoin d'esprit que de corps, ... l'importune guêpe la Condamine, Mairan le protecteur né de tous les plats sujets ... et probablement le bas et insolent Duclos, qui a dans tout ceci une conduite bien tortueuse" (Best. 8895, 9 March 1761). The philosophes then succeeded in acquiring one of their own, Saurin, and one sympathetic to their cause, the Cardinal de Rohan-Guéménée, later that year. Yet, d'Alembert was still dissatisfied, be-

---

[27] Wilson, pp. 308-309.

cause Marmontel, who had become Voltaire's favorite candidate as well, was still outside the Academy. On 9 April 1761, he reported to Voltaire: "Ainsi nous avons eu sept places vacantes à la fois, et nous n'avons pas choisi le seul homme qu'il nous convenoit de prendre" (Best. 8948).

Marmontel was finally elected in 1763. His entrance into the Academy marks the beginning of the reign of the philosophes in the Company. The following four members to be admitted were all sponsored by d'Alembert's faction: Thomas, elected in 1766, Condillac, in 1768, Saint-Lambert and Loménie de Brienne, Bishop of Toulouse in 1770. By then the philosophes had securely established themselves in the Company. The members of their clan were the most active and the most talented among the Academicians; they not only dominated, but threatened to take full control of the Academy.

Voltaire, during these years, exerted a minor influence on the choices the Academy made. He took a more active part in only one election, in 1763, when Marmontel presented himself as a candidate. The young playwright paid a visit to Voltaire earlier that year and was encouraged by the patriarch to seek entrance into the Academy. Voltaire suggested that he first attract the body's attention by entering its yearly poetry contest. Marmontel did and won first prize with his *Epître aux Poètes*. When a vacancy occurred at the death of Bougainville in June, Voltaire urged his friend: "Voilà le froid Bougainville mort, mon cher ami. Il faut que vous réchauffiez l'Académie. Je vais écrire à tous mes amis" (Best. 10481, 7 July 1763). The success of the election seemed assured to Voltaire, for he added: "J'ose croire même que vous n'aurez point de concurrent." He was also encouraged in his optimism by Thieriot, who reported: "Jusqu'à présent l'Election ne regarde que Marmontel" (Best. 10511, 30 July 1763). The situation in Paris was not as favorable as Voltaire imagined it. Nevertheless, thanks to his own persistence and to the help of his friends, d'Alembert and Duclos, Marmontel became one of the forty Immortals on 24 November 1763.[28] A few days after Marmontel's reception into the Academy, Voltaire expressed his delight to Damilaville: "Tout annonce, Dieu mercy, un siècle philosophique" (Best. 10780, 4 January 1764).

---

[28] The details of Marmontel's candidacy are recounted in his memoirs: Marmontel, *Œuvres Complètes* (Paris: Verdière, 1818-1819), I, 439-464.

Voltaire was satisfied with the gains the *frères* were making in the Academy and observed with great pleasure the growing force of philosophes in the Company. In 1770 he remarked: "Les places de l'académie deviennent de jour en jour plus prétieuses, et plus dignes des principaux citoiens de Paris" (Best. 15660, to Dorat, 1 October 1770). He followed the elections with interest and occasionally made recommendations to his confrères and to persons of influence, but for several years he did not see the need to intervene in the business of the Academy. This placid attitude came to an end in December 1770, when the *président* de Brosses presented himself as a candidate for a vacant seat.

The *président* had already been considering Academic honors for several years and had acquired by 1770 a stature and a reputation that seemed to amply justify his candidacy. Towards the end of the year three vacancies occurred within a short time and de Brosses's friends inside the Academy thought the moment to be propitious for their plans. The *président*'s chances seemed excellent. They were suddenly dashed by Voltaire's forceful and unexpected intervention. On 10 December 1770 he wrote to d'Alembert: "On dit aussi que le président Debrosses se présente.... Il a eu un procédé bien vilain avec moi, et j'ai encore la lettre dans laquelle il m'écrit en mots couverts que, si je le poursuis, il pourra me dénoncer comme auteur d'ouvrages suspects que je n'ai certainement point faits. Je puis produire ces belles choses à l'académie, et je ne crois pas qu'un tel homme vous convienne" (Best. 15788). Voltaire had been involved in legal disputes with de Brosses for a number of years. He now revealed that in order to avoid a lawsuit, the *président* had threatened to use blackmail. For the next few months, Voltaire led an energetic campaign intended to discredit de Brosses in the eyes of the philosophes. He wrote to his friends d'Argental, Marmontel, Thomas, Duclos, even to Richelieu, who had become one of the leaders of the *dévots* inside the Academy and who was sponsoring de Brosses. The accusation Voltaire brought against the président was serious and seemed to imply that all philosophes were threatened. Writing to Duclos he described de Brosses as "un homme qui menace les gens de lettres d'être leur délateur" (Best. 15834, 24 December 1770).

While attacking de Brosses, Voltaire also took pains to recommend other suitable candidates. When yet another chair was vacated in 1771, he even addressed himself to the entire Academy in order to recommend the poet Delille (Best. 16023, 4 March 1771). Some of his choices would have been surprising under different circumstances; the important thing at the moment, however, was to prevent an election. In writing to d'Alembert, he recommended such obscure figures as Marin and Caperonnier (Best. 15826). Another time he inquired: "Ne pourriez vous pas avoir quelque espèce de grand seigneur?" (Best. 15814). He was also prepared to take the most drastic measures, as he warned his disciple: "Je passe le Rubicon, pour chasser le nasillonneur délateur et persécuteur; et je déclare que je serai obligé de renoncer à ma place, si on lui en donne une" (Best. 15840, 28 December 1770). [29] De Brosses finally realized that the obstacle in his path to the Academy was unsurmountable, and desisted, never to present himself again.

Voltaire had been successful not only in convincing his friends that de Brosses was undesirable, but even in influencing erstwhile supporters of de Brosses, such as Foncemagne, to abandon the *président*. [30] Voltaire's friends had readily acceeded to his arguments and had complied with the patriarch's wishes. More difficult to understand are the motives behind Voltaire's unrelenting campaign. The oversimple explanation usually put forth by historians who have studied the de Brosses-Voltaire relationship does little more than repeat Sainte-Beuve, who first observed that "Le Président de Brosses, pour n'avoir pas voulu faire cadeau à Voltaire des quatorze moules de bois ... ne put jamais être de l'Académie française." [31] Voltaire has been condemned unanimously by these critics who speak of his "laideurs et ... vices de l'âme" [32] and of his "duplicité inouïe." [33] The entire history of the relationship between the two men is especially complex since it involves the financial interests of the two parties. Voltaire rented Tournay from de Brosses and had signed a life-long lease of the property in 1758. The landlord and the tenant had since then been

---

[29] De Brosses apparently had a pronounced nasal tone when speaking, whence the nickname used by Voltaire.

[30] Buffon, *Correspondance inédite de Buffon* (Paris: Hachette, 1860), I, 131.

[31] Sainte-Beuve, "Voltaire et le Président de Brosses ou une intrigue académique au XVIIIe siècle," *Causeries du Lundi*, VII (Paris: Garnier Frères, 1852), p. 123. See also Desnoiresterres, pp. 121-154; Brunel, pp. 210-216.

[32] Sainte-Beuve, p. 124.

[33] Brunel, p. 212.

involved in numerous disputes and litigations. The affair of the "Quatorze moules de bois" was one of the earliest quarrels and broke out in 1761. By 1768, Voltaire nursed a bitter resentment towards the *président*. He referred to the time of his acquaintance with de Brosses as "dix années de vexations et de chagrin" (Best. 14230, to Fyot de la Marche, 26 August 1768).

Voltaire had several grounds for complaint against the *président*. The most serious vexations were caused by the property of Tournay which was financially unprofitable and had become a burden to Voltaire: "The woodlands of Tournay would have kept him warm in winter, and would have also yielded him a profit; but President de Brosses, before leasing the property to Voltaire for life, had already over-exploited them, and he cleverly left to his tenant the plantings rather than the cuttings." In addition, "a heavy tax which Voltaire was forced to pay for the leasing of Tournay made that acquisition an even worse bargain than at first appeared." [34] Speaking of Tournay in 1768, Voltaire remarked: "Je l'ai achetée fort cher et je n'en ai presque rien retiré. J'ai fait beaucoup trop de dépenses à cette maison que je n'ai jamais habitée" (Best. 14459, to Jean-Louis Sales, 11 January 1769). At the time, he was attempting to change certain clauses of his contract with de Brosses, which he deemed highly unfavorable to himself and to his heirs. It was during these negotiations that Voltaire had received the letter which provided him with his most effective argument in keeping the *président* out of the Academy.

The famous letter has naturally been described as a pure invention on Voltaire's part and all of his references to it, characterized as lies and calumnies. Voltaire indicated in a letter, written on 2 January 1771, that d'Alembert had already seen de Brosses's threats the previous year, while visiting the patriarch at Ferney: "Un homme d'un rare mérite, qui était chez moi, vit cette lettre et en fut très affligé. Il en a parlé en dernier lieu, lorsqu'il s'est agi de l'Académie française" (Best. 15907, to Legouz de Gerland). Pure lies, according to some. D'Alembert had neither heard of the letter nor seen it before de Brosses's candidacy: "Il a si peu lu la lettre en question, que Voltaire lui en parle pour la première fois, le 10 décembre, en apprenant la candidature du président ... la prétendue lettre, il ne la connaît pas;

---

[34] Norman Lewis Torrey, *The Spirit of Voltaire* (New York: Columbia University Press, 1938), pp. 191 and 194.

elle n'existe pas." [35] First of all, the tone Voltaire uses in his letter of 10 December does not prove that he is speaking of the matter for the first time; it can be considered the tone of a reminder as well. Secondly, before d'Alembert had received this letter he had written to Voltaire:

> Je vous ai déjà averti il y a quelques jours, mon cher et illustre maître, que le président de Brosses est sur les rangs pour l'académie... nous sommes menacés de cette platte acquisition, si nous ne faisons pas l'impossible pour la parer. Or vous saurez que le grand promoteur de ce plat président, est le doucereux Foncemagne, qui peut-être craindroit de vous désobliger, s'il savoit que vous serez offensé d'un pareil choix... Foncemagne... ignore aussi vraisemblablement que vous avez à vous plaindre du président de Brosses. (Best. 15793, 12 December 1770).

The statements "vous serez offensé d'un pareil choix" and "vous avez à vous plaindre du président de Brosses" have been interpreted as indicating that "d'Alembert ne connaît jusqu'alors d'autre histoire que celle des quatorze moules de bois." [36] One would expect, then, to see a change in the force and in the choice of expressions in d'Alembert's next letter, written after he had been informed of the *président*'s menaces by Voltaire's letter of 10 December. The tone, however, is identical and the expressions strangely similar: "Mais un confrère qu'il faut bien nous garder d'acquérir c'est ce plat et ridicule président de Brosses, dont vous avez tant à vous plaindre; vous feriez bien ... d'écrire ... combien vous seriez offensé d'un pareil choix" (Best. 15832, to Voltaire, 22 (?) December 1770). [37] D'Alembert's letter shows no trace of shock or even surprise, on the contrary, it has the sound of a recommendation that is repeated only as a reminder.

There is yet another piece of evidence pointing to the existence of this letter and leading us to think that it was written sometime in the first part of 1768. [38] On 24 September 1768, Voltaire wrote to a

---

[35] Brunel, p. 213. A passage from this letter of 10 December from Voltaire to d'Alembert has been quoted on p. 80.
[36] *Ibid.*
[37] Besterman, apparently, is not entirely certain of the exact date of the letter. Its contents indicate clearly, however, that it was written after the reception of Voltaire's letter of 10 December.
[38] Besterman suggests (Best. 15788, note 5) that Best. 14217 (Voltaire to de Brosses, 18 August 1768) was perhaps written in response to the letter

colleague of de Brosses, the *président* de Ruffey, and complained of his landlord in the following terms: "Vous et Mr le Gout frémiriez d'horreur si je vous informais du procédé que Mr De Brosses a eu en dernier lieu. Promettez moi le secret, et je vous dirai de quoi il s'agit ... il me menace de me persécuter. La chose est difficile, mais l'idée en est abominable, et c'est le comble de l'infamie" (Best. 14258). Even granting Voltaire's tendency to exaggerate, we can assume these statements are referring to something more serious than a dispute over some wood or over a contract.

For Voltaire, these threats were especially serious because they came at a time when he was particularly sensitive to the dangers of persecution. The horror of the chevalier de La Barre's death was still fresh in his mind and threats to denounce the philosophe as the author of irreligious works had an ominous ring since he had been directly implicated in the La Barre affair: a copy of his *Dictionnaire philosophique* had been found among the young man's belongings. The names of the chevalier and of other famous victims of fanaticism come up regularly in the letters Voltaire wrote at the time and show us the old philosophe obsessed with the question of man's injustice and cruelty toward his fellow man. On 30 August 1769, for example, he confided to d'Argental: "Je ne vois de tous côtés que les injustices les plus barbares; Lally et son baillon, Sirven, Calas, Martin, Le Chevalier de La Barre se présentent quelquefois à moi dans mes rêves.... J'ai toujours la fièvre le 24 du mois d'auguste ... je tombe en défaillance le 14 May" (Best. 14871). [39] The concern for personal safety was closely associated with the memory of these distant and recent persecutions. The connection is made clear by the letters Voltaire wrote to his friends to explain his Easter Communion of 1768 and 1769. Thus, he justified his actions to d'Alembert stating that "on ne me traitera pas comme le chevalier de la Barre" (Best. 14699, 4 June 1769).

Voltaire's forceful reaction to de Brosses's candidacy, shocking if we accept a nine year old quarrel over some cut wood as the motive, becomes intelligible in the light of these circumstances. Voltaire was extremely careful not to antagonize anyone at the moment, not even

---

in question. In Best. 14217 Voltaire states that he is answering de Brosses's letter of 10 May 1768.

[39] 24 August is St. Bartholomew's Day and Henri IV was assassinated by the religious fanatic Ravaillac on 14 May.

de Brosses, and a denunciation of the président is often followed by a plea for discretion in his letters. This recommendation to d'Alembert is typical: "Mais tâchez que MM Duclos, Thomas, Marmontel, Saurin, Voisenon, gardent le secret" (Best. 15826, 21 December 1770). Voltaire even took pains to deny that he was engaged in any activity intended to discredit de Brosses. On 27 February 1771 he informed the *président* de Ruffey: "On a persuadé à Mr De Brosses que je m'étais opposé à son élection, parce que j'avais écrit plusieurs Lettres en faveur de Mr Gaillard. Mais je le prie de considérer que j'avais écrit ces Lettres longtemps avant que j'eusse apris que Mr De Brosses voulût être nôtre confrère. Il nous fera certainement bien de l'honneur à la première occasion" (Best. 16016). This is indeed duplicity, but it must be remembered that de Brosses represented a real threat to Voltaire and that the latter was simply resorting to an old and reliable defense mechanism, a tactic that had become second nature to him: "His lying and hypocrisy... constituted an accepted, systematic, reasoned method. The necessity of such duplicity was early impressed upon him by his many exiles and flights from justice, by two sojourns in the Bastille, and by the bitter enmities he had made in the opposing camp." [40]

The need to adopt a defensive stance was not caused by de Brosses alone. A mood that was highly unfavorable to the philosophes had recently set in and the members of the group were fearful of new persecutions, especially since the publication of d'Holbach's *Système de la nature* in 1770. The appearance of this treatise on atheism caused a split in the philosophe party and led to the formation of a Voltaire-d'Alembert faction representing a moderate and conciliatory point of view and opposing the more intransigent Diderot-d'Holbach group. [41] Voltaire had generally been respectful of the State and defended the point of view that "c'est l'intérêt du roy, c'est celui de l'état que les philosophes gouvernent la société" (Best. 10595, Voltaire to Helvétius, 15 September 1763). He now found himself in an ironic situation. His incensed reaction to the *Système de la nature*: "Ils attaquent à la fois Dieu, le Diable, les grands et les prêtres. Que leur

---

[40] Torrey, *The Spirit of Voltaire*, p. 122.
[41] See John N. Pappas, "Voltaire et la Guerre Civile Philosophique," *Revue d'Histoire littéraire de la France*, 61e année, No. 4 (Oct.-Dec., 1961), 525-549. Also his *Voltaire and d'Alembert*, Chapter V.

restera-t-il?" (Best. 15531, to d'Alembert, 27 July 1770) had caused him to become a defender of religion. Some of his contemporaries did not fail to express their amusement. The abbé Galiani commented: "C'est bien plaisant qu'on soit parvenu à un point que Voltaire paraisse modéré dans ses opinions, et qu'il se flatte d'être compté parmi les protecteurs de la religion, et qu'il faille, au lieu de le persécuter, le protéger et l'encourager." [42] Nevertheless, as he explained to d'Alembert, he could not associate himself with the extreme tactics of the Encyclopedists: "Un grand mal moral qui pourra bien aller jusqu'au phisique, c'est la publication du Système de la nature. Ce livre a rendu tous les philosophes exécrables aux yeux du Roi et de toute la cour. ... L'éditeur de ce fatal ouvrage a perdu la philosophie à jamais dans l'esprit de tous les magistrats et de tous les pères de famille qui sentent combien l'athéisme peut être dangereux pour la société" (Best. 15718, 2 November 1770). D'Alembert fully agreed with his *maître* and the two philosophes decided to adopt a conduct intended to guarantee their personal safety and to rehabilitate the image of their party: "Henceforth the furthering of the cause takes the form of seconding and defending the Philosophes in the Académie française." [43]

Inside the Academy, d'Alembert and his friends were beginning to meet with a resolute opposition, as their influence grew and threatened to dominate entirely the life and the decisions of the Company. The faction of the *dévots* had been observing with mounting alarm the transformation of the Academy and the increasing use of its functions as vehicles of free-thinking ideas. For one, the subjects of the Academy's annual contest in eloquence and in poetry had been radically changed. The *concours de poésie*, which had until 1750 sung the praises of Louis XIV, admitted topics of the poet's own choosing. The essays presented to the *concours d'éloquence* had formerly taken the form of theological treatises. Thanks to Duclos they had changed to "les éloges des hommes illustres de la nation dans tous les genres, sans acception de rang, de titre ni de naissance." [44] The

---

[42] Abbé F. Galiani, *Lettres à Mme d'Epinay* (Paris: Charpentier, 1903), I, 364.

[43] Pappas, *Voltaire and d'Alembert*, p. 128. John Pappas suggests also that d'Alembert and Voltaire decided upon this new tactic during the geometer's visit at Ferney and determined at that time to break with the Diderot-d'Holbach faction (*Ibid.*, p. 118).

[44] Duclos, I, 581.

direct effect of these transformations had become clear to everyone: "C'était faire de l'éloquence académique — c'est à dire au fond de l'éloquence philosophique — un instrument d'éducation nationale." [45] A disciple of the philosophes, Antoine-Léonard Thomas, had become a master of the genre and was rewarded with a chair in the Academy principally for his oratorical accomplishments. He was also to bring upon the Academy its first difficulties with the government.

In 1770, at the reception of the Archbishop of Toulouse, the discourse Thomas made in answering the newly admitted member contained allusions to the recent condemnation by the *Parlement* of certain philosophic works. Séguier, who was *premier avocat général* of the *Parlement*, had delivered a *Réquisitoire* demanding the public burning of these works, which included d'Holbach's *Système de la nature* and Voltaire's *Dieu et les hommes*. The discourse was interpreted as an attack directed against Séguier, one of the leaders of the *dévots* inside the Academy. This in turn led to the examination of an *Eloge de Marc-Aurèle* Thomas had delivered two weeks earlier and Bachaumont reported: "*L'Eloge de Marc-Aurèle* fait un bruit du diable. On trouve bien extraordinaire que, dans le sanctuaire de l'Académie, protégée par le roi, dans son palais, un membre de cette compagnie ait osé avancer les propositions les plus hardies, fronder le gouvernement actuel avec tant de dureté, et inculper, ce semble, tous les ministres, par des apostrophes et des allusions dont on ne peut méconnaître le sens et les rapports." [46] The Chancellor Maupeou prohibited the printing of the two discourses and Thomas was forbidden to speak in public sessions of the Academy for two years. The Academy as a body was implicated in the affair; as a result, "de ce jour cessèrent les relations, jusqu'alors faciles et pacifiques, de l'Académie avec le pouvoir." [47]

Other difficulties followed, and at every vexation the Academy endured, the philosophes saw clearly that the attack was aimed at them. In 1771 the Academy was reprimanded by the King himself. An *Eloge de Fénelon* by La Harpe which had won the annual prize,

---

[45] Etienne Micard, *Un Ecrivain Académique au XVIIIe siècle: Antoine-Léonard Thomas* (Paris: Champion, 1924), p. 122.

[46] Louis Petit de Bachaumont, *Mémoires secrets, 1762-1787* (Londres: John Adamson, 1777-1789), V, 159.

[47] Brunel, p. 200.

had scandalized the devout and provoked the Archbishops of Reims and of Paris to denounce the work. The Company was reminded to respect an old statute which required all writers competing for the prize in eloquence to get their works approved by two doctors of the Sorbonne. In relating these events to his *maître,* d'Alembert concluded bitterly: "Il faudra pourtant désormais se soumettre à ce joug" (Best. 16348, 7 October 1771). Voltaire was speaking for the whole philosophe group when he wrote to d'Argental: "Le soufflet donné à la Harpe et à notre académie, est tout chaud sur ma joue" (Best. 16351, 11 October 1771).

The philosophes had no choice but to submit if they wished to preserve the Academy. They were reminded of their responsibilities towards the State and their dependence on their protector by an unprecedented letter from the King which was read in the session of 6 April 1772:

> Plus l'Académie française est sous ma protection et direction immédiate, et plus je dois exiger la régularité la plus exacte de tous ses membres; de plus je leur ordonne d'apporter l'attention la plus sévère et la plus impartiale à l'examen des pièces qui concourent au prix, afin qu'ils s'épargnent l'humiliation de voir supprimer ce qu'ils auroient témérairement approuvé. Mon intention est aussi qu'ils ayent encore plus d'égards, s'il est possible, aux principes et aux mœurs dans le choix des sujets proposés pour être admis à l'Académie, afin de ne pas se mettre dans le cas d'éprouver un refus qui ne pourroit que leur être désagréable. (Registres, III, 306)

The statement was all the more significant since Duclos had recently died and the Academy was to elect a new secretary on 9 April. As everyone had expected, d'Alembert was chosen, and to gain the King's assent, a delegate was sent to inform the royal protector of the election; the consent of the King was not required for such an election but was sought in an apparent attempt at conciliation. Louis XV was evidently satisfied with this show of deference and approved the new secretary. For d'Alembert's party, this latest success made up for the recent setbacks and Voltaire sounded a note of optimism in writing to Condorcet: "J'ai été tenté de me mettre dans une grosse colère à l'occasion de tout ce qui s'est passé à l'académie française. Mais quand je considère que Mr D'Alembert a bien voulu être nôtre secrétaire perpétuel, je suis de bonne humeur, parce que je suis sûr qu'il mettra les choses sur un très bon pied. Les ouragans passent, et la philosophie demeure" (Best. 16684, 11 May 1772).

Voltaire's optimism was premature, for yet another adversity had fallen on the Academy. The King had just vetoed the elections of Suard and Delille, two candidates of the philosophe party chosen by the Academy on 7 May. It turned out that the King's actions had been prompted by Richelieu, who later found it necessary to deny his insidious role to his fellow Academicians (Registres, III, 310). Eventually, after he was shown that the condemnation was unjust, the King rescinded his decision and Suard and Delille were elected anew in 1774. Nevertheless, even though the final outcome of this confrontation had been favorable for the Academy, the Company had been reminded once more of its dependent status. The philosophes had been made to understand that their superiority in number did not give them unlimited freedom and that their actions would have to be guided by a policy of compromise.

For Voltaire, the harassment his friends endured inside the Academy was but another sign of the times. It was simply another manifestation of the prevalent antiphilosophic mood. It was also an additional argument to support a growing conviction that the Academy could never become an exclusive club for free-thinkers. It is significant to note that after his campaign against de Brosses, Voltaire never again made a serious attempt to influence an election. He did continue to indicate his preferences and expressed support notably for two candidates, La Harpe and Condorcet,[48] but generally speaking, the old philosophe's attitude suggests a desire to avoid serious conflicts with his fellow Academicians.

The conservative and conciliatory attitude Voltaire eventually adopted with regard to the factional struggles inside the Academy does not really come as a surprise. First of all, some of the relationships he cultivated had often made him suspect as a defender of the philosophic cause. We have already mentioned that his indulgent attitude toward Palissot was severely criticized by the *encyclopédistes*. Inside the Academy, his continuing friendship with some of the more tenacious anti-philosophes, in particular with Richelieu and d'Olivet, was frequently condemned by d'Alembert. Voltaire was well aware of his

---

[48] La Harpe was elected in 1776 and Condorcet only after Voltaire's death in 1781.

friend's disapproval in this matter and occasionally found the situation rather humorous. Thus, in 1770 the *premier avocat général* of the *Parlement* of Paris had just visited Voltaire at Ferney when d'Alembert arrived. The patriarch noted that his disciple "arriva à Ferney dans le moment où M. Séguier en partait," and added, "J'aurais bien voulu qu'ils eussent dîné ensemble, mais dieu n'a pas permis cette plaisante scène" (Best. 15655, to Michel de Chabanon, 28 September 1770). The difference in attitudes between the two friends can be illustrated by comparing the comments each one offered at the time of d'Olivet's death. When Voltaire found out the abbé was seriously ill, he wrote: "L'abbé d'Olivet est un bon homme, et je l'ai toujours aimé" (Best. 14239, to d'Alembert, 2 September 1768). After his former master's death he added: "Nous avons perdu un très bon académicien dans l'abbé d'Olivet" (Best. 14319, to La Harpe, 31 October 1768). D'Alembert, on the other hand, remarked a few days later: "C'était un passable académicien, mais un bien mauvais confrère, qui haïssoit tout le monde, et qui, entre nous, ne vous aimait pas plus qu'un autre" (Best. 14348, to Voltaire, 12 November 1768).

D'Alembert was even more critical of Voltaire's friendly relations with Richelieu and in general objected to the patriarch's courting the favor of the *puissances*; John Pappas notes that "the divergence in policy on this question had never really been resolved between them." [49] Voltaire, however, found it impossible to consider these ties in a simple context of a philosophe-*dévot* conflict and occasionally defended himself against d'Alembert's criticisms. In 1769, he protested: "Par dieu vous êtes bien injuste de me reprocher mes ménagements pour gens puissants que je n'ay connus jadis que pour gens aimables, à qui j'ay les dernières obligations, et qui même m'ont deffendu contre les monstres. En quoy pui'je me plaindre d'eux?" (Best. 14464, to d'Alembert, 13 January 1769). In the case of Richelieu, Voltaire had various grounds for complaint. We have mentioned only a few of Richelieu's little treacheries. Some of his actions went against the interests of Voltaire outside the sphere of the Academy as well. Voltaire nevertheless seemed to take very lightly the vexations inflicted by his "héros." On 25 June 1770 he wrote to Richelieu: "Je vois que vous faites la guerre aux philosophes ne pouvant plus la faire aux Anglais et aux Alle-

---

[49] Pappas, *Voltaire and d'Alembert*, p. 137.

mands" (Best. 15436), and on 11 July: "Mon héros en me caressant d'une main, m'égratigne un peu de l'autre selon sa louable coutume" (Best. 15490).

As the *maréchal*'s campaign against the philosophes intensified and as d'Alembert sent new accounts of Richelieu's misdeeds to Ferney, Voltaire's mood changed momentarily, and there were occasions when the old philosophe sounded bitter (Best. 16766 and 17297). By 1775, however, Voltaire had apparently forgiven, for in his letter of 1 October to Richelieu we read: "Permettez moi de vous dire que vous êtes un peu trop difficile sur nôtre académie dont vous êtes le Doyen, et dont il n'apartenait qu'à vous d'être le soutien et le véritable protecteur. Je vous ouvre mon cœur. J'ai été très affligé, et je le suis encor, que vous aiez un peu gourmandé des hommes libres, qui pensent et qui parlent, qui même ont une grande influence sur l'opinion publique" (Best. 18558). Finally in 1778, when the two old friends met again, they settled down for an amicable discussion of the roles in Voltaire's latest play, *Irène*.[50]

This tolerant attitude towards a few enemies of the philosophes was reinforced by a growing concern to avoid persecution. On 15 April 1769, Voltaire had given the following explanation for his latest Holy Communion to Richelieu: "Je dois d'abord vous dire, comme au chef de l'académie que j'ai fait à l'égard de la religion tout ce que la bienséance exige d'un homme qui est d'un corps à qui le mépris de ces bienséances pourrait attirer une partie des reproches que l'on eût fait à ma mémoire" (Best. 14615). Voltaire's friendly relations with a few *dévot* members of the Academy, his increased regard for certain "bienséances," were factors that led the patriarch to abandon his polemic activities related to the Academy. They help to explain the accommodating mood Voltaire showed in the seventies.

Even during the years of intense campaigning Voltaire had lacked the unswerving determination apparent in the actions of d'Alembert, for obvious reasons. Voltaire was far from Paris and had many other matters on his mind. He could also feel secure in the thought that d'Alembert was always there at the Academy to defend the interests of the philosophes. There was, however, a basic difference in the attitudes the two men held with regard to the Academy. It was simply

---

[50] Desnoiresterres, VIII, 208.

impossible for the patriarch to achieve the single-mindedness in his aims that was evident in d'Alembert's attitude. The geometer wished to change the Academy into a stronghold for his party and considered anyone opposed to his projects an enemy. Voltaire was usually more tolerant of his fellow Academicians. While he had supported with enthusiasm the conquest of the Academy, he had never lost sight of a consideration that had always remained primordial in his understanding of the Academy's role. For Voltaire, the Academy had always been, and still remained, even under the banner of the philosophes, a citadel of letters.

Chapter IV

THE CITADEL OF LETTERS

The reasons for which Voltaire had wanted to enter the Academy have already been examined. We have seen that he valued highly the distinction of belonging to a company that had been instituted to foster the language and the letters of France. For Voltaire, this role had always remained the Academy's principal *raison d'être,* even while the philosophes were struggling to dominate the Company in the sixties. In writing to d'Alembert in 1763, Voltaire noted that French language and culture had penetrated almost all of the courts of Europe, and added: "Ce n'est pourtant ni à messieurs du Parlement, ni à messieurs des convulsions, ni à nos généraux, ni à nos premiers commis qu'on doit cette petite distinction. Une douzaine d'êtres pensants, à la tête desquels vous êtes, empêche que la France ne soit la dernière des nations" (Best. 10363, 1 May 1763). For Voltaire, each new philosophe addition to the body of Immortals was a gain for the cause of letters. He applauded, for example, Marmontel's election: "Voilà notre académie bien fortifiée.... Le jour de votre réception sera un grand jour pour les belles lettres" (Best. 10693, to Marmontel, 1 December 1763). Speaking of the Academy in 1767, Voltaire proudly announced: "Elle est à présent sur un pied plus honorable que jamais, elle rend les lettres respectables" (Best. 13052, to Palissot, 13 February 1767).

While giving credit to the philosophes for having restored the prestige of the Academy, Voltaire nonetheless drew a distinction between the two causes he was defending, the progress of Enlightenment on the one hand, and the advancement of literature on the other. He had already underlined this difference in 1735, in a letter to Cideville:

"Les Belles-lettres périssent à vue d'œil. Ce n'est pas que je suis fâché que la philosophie soit cultivée, mais je ne voudrois pas qu'elle devînt un tiran qui exclût tout le reste" (Best. 838, 16 April 1735). As he saw *la philosophie* gaining and literature deteriorating, the duality became more pronounced in his mind: "This consciousness of literary decadence forms perhaps the most constantly reiterated theme in his critical thought."[1] Statements such as: "La philosophie gagne et les arts se perdent" (Best. 15196, to La Harpe, 2 March 1770), and "Il y a une distance immense entre les talents et l'esprit philosophique qui s'est répendu chez toutes les nations" (Best. 15713, to Grimm, 1 November 1770), occur with growing frequency in letters written during the last twenty years of his life. At the same time, the Academy represented a positive force for Voltaire, an influence that had the power to uphold high standards of taste in French letters. In the final chapter of the *Précis du siècle de Louis XV*, written in 1768, Voltaire referred to the decline of the arts in France and stated: "C'est contre cette décadence que l'Académie française lutte continuellement; elle préserve le bon goût d'une ruine totale, en n'accordant du moins des prix qu'à ce qui est écrit avec quelque pureté et en réprouvant tout ce qui pêche par le style" (Moland, XV, 439). The same year, Voltaire sent a copy of *Le siècle de Louis XIV* to the Academy and in writing to its secretary, Duclos, he explained: "J'ai l'honneur de vous adresser le siècle de Louis XIV que vous voulez bien présenter à l'Académie. C'est le siècle du bon goût, et j'ai dit expressément que ce siècle ne commença qu'à la fondation de l'Académie française, je dis à la fin qu'elle le soutient encore" (Best. 14395, 8 December 1768). Voltaire was thus reaffirming the convictions he had expressed almost twenty years before.[2] He expressed his respect for Academies in general two years later in the article "Académie" of the *Dictionnaire philosophique*: "Les académies sont aux universités ce que l'âge mûr est à l'enfance, ce que l'art de bien penser est à la grammaire, ce que la politesse est aux premières leçons de la civilité" (Moland, XVII, 50). At the same time, Voltaire gave particular credit to the French Academy: "L'Académie française a rendu de grands services à la langue" (Moland, XVII, 53). As late as 1777, at a time when the

---

[1] David Williams, *Voltaire: Literary Critic*, Studies on Voltaire and the Eighteenth Century, XLVIII (Geneva: Droz, 1966), 87.

[2] These passages of *Le siècle de Louis XIV* have already been quoted in Chapter II, p. 67.

Academy was increasingly criticized for the sterility of its preoccupations, Voltaire defended the merits of the Institution: "C'est un corps plus utile qu'on ne pense, en ne faisant rien, parce qu'il sera toujours le dépôt du bon goût qui se perd totalement en France. Il faut le laisser subsister comme ces anciens monuments qui ne servaient qu'à montrer le chemin" (Best. 19723, to the comte de Schomberg, 2 November 1777). This confidence in the role of the Academy was reinforced by the fact that Voltaire himself had endeavored for many years to augment the prestige of the Company.

Voltaire contributed to the renown of the Academy in two distinct manners. The glory of the Institution was first of all enhanced by the very circumstance of Voltaire's membership. The Academy gained even more from this situation through the deliberate efforts of d'Alembert. In his campaign to build the reputation of the philosophe party, the geometer took advantage of every opportunity to emphasize the merits of his "brothers," and of Voltaire especially. He had begun in 1760 "by giving a forceful eulogy of Voltaire at the Académie française in his *Réflexions sur la poésie*," and renewed his praises in 1761 in his *Réflexions sur l'histoire*.[3] On 11 August 1770 he read to the Academy a letter he had received from Frederick (Best. 15535), which was in effect a tribute to Voltaire. The following day d'Alembert announced with evident pleasure: "Je lus hier à l'académie française la lettre du Roi de Prusse, et elle arrêta d'une voix unanime que cette lettre seroit insérée dans ses registres, comme un monument honorable pour vous et pour les lettres. Je donnerai à ce monument si flatteur pour vous, et même pour nous tous, toute la publicité qui dépendra de moi" (Best. 15561, to Voltaire, 12 August 1770). Voltaire thanked the Academy for this distinction and stated his view that "elle n'a considéré que l'honneur qui rejaillit sur la littérature dont elle est le modèle et la protectrice" (Best. 15584, to Duclos, 20 August 1770).

There were other Academicians who contributed to Voltaire's reputation in a similar manner. The abbé d'Olivet apparently communicated to the Academy a long letter in which Voltaire discussed various questions pertaining to French language and letters (Best. 12914), for d'Alembert wrote on 26 January 1767: "Nous avons lu hier en pleine académie votre lettre à l'abbé d'Olivet, qui nous a fait très grand plaisir" (Best. 12988). A few years later, Voltaire's name

---

[3] Pappas, *Voltaire and d'Alembert*, pp. 21, 26, and 27.

was beginning to appear regularly in discourses pronounced on the days when new members were received into the Academy. Reporting on the latest election, Suzanne Necker wrote in 1775: "C'est dans ce temple dédié à l'immortalité qu'on entend à chaque mort l'éloge assez mince de l'académicien qui n'est plus, et l'éloge toujours applaudi de notre Homère, et de notre Sophocle" (Best. 18340, to Voltaire, 2 May 1775). D'Alembert could only be pleased upon seeing that others, though perhaps for different reasons, were adopting a conduct he had initiated.

For d'Alembert, literary productions and literary merit represented mainly propaganda material for furthering "the cause," and "a candidate's philosophical outlook was a more important qualification for Academy honours than literary achievement." [4] In this respect, his point of view differed greatly from that of Voltaire. Although the *maître* never reproached his disciple for this attitude, he could not refrain, upon occasion, from adopting an ironic tone when referring to d'Alembert's untiring struggle to acquire right-minded candidates. In 1770, when the Archbishop of Toulouse had been elected, Voltaire wrote: "On dit que vous nous donnez pour confrère monsieur l'archevêque de Toulouse, qui passe pour une bête de votre façon, très bien disciplinée par vous" (Best. 15391, to d'Alembert, 11 June 1770). In general, however, Voltaire valued d'Alembert's efforts to change the Academy and generously praised the geometer, as, for example, in 1775: "Vraiment vous avez ressuscité notre académie; elle était morte sans vous" (Best. 18241, 26 February 1775). In addition, Voltaire appreciated the backing he received from his disciple in Paris. Always eager to enhance the literary credit of the philosophes, d'Alembert usually gave his full support to the literary projects his master undertook under the aegis of the Academy.

These personal projects, added to his participation in collective tasks, constituted Voltaire's second contribution to the prestige of the French Academy. His first attempt at collaboration took place in 1760, when Duclos invited him to do the letter "T" for the fourth edition of the *Dictionnaire de l'Académie*. [5] Voltaire was happy to comply and answered on 11 August: "Je suis entièrement à vos ordres pour le

---

[4] Grimsley, p. 105.

[5] The previous editions had appeared in 1694, 1718 and 1740. This latest edition had been started thanks principally to the efforts of Duclos.

dictionnaire de l'académie: je vous remercie de l'honneur que vous voulez bien me faire." He congratulated Duclos on his plan for the new edition, remarking that previously, "on s'était fait une loi de ne point citer, mais un dictionnaire sans citations est un squelette" (Best. 8378). Voltaire illustrated his words accordingly, but in the process, the examples acquired a very special Voltairean flavor. The uses of the verb *tenir*, for example, were elucidated with the following samples: "Il s'en *tient* à l'Evangile et rejette la tradition" and "On dit que Siméon Stylite se *tint* plusieurs années sur une jambe. Les grues se *tiennent* souvent sur une patte" (Moland, XX, 495 and 493). Voltaire's conception of a dictionary was too original for the Academy to accept; as a result, the 1762 edition of the *Dictionnaire de l'Académie* appeared without a single line of Voltaire's work.[6] Voltaire showed understandable disapprobation in evaluating the Academy's work: "On n'est pas content de notre dictionnaire, on le trouve sec, décharné, incomplet, en comparaison de ceux de Madrid et de Florence" (Best. 9668, to Bernis, 26 May 1762). When sometime later the dictionary had turned out to be a financial disaster, he observed with a certain satisfaction: "J'avais bien prévu, quand je vis le dictionnaire de l'académie, que le Libraire ferait banqueroute" (Best. 10594, to Damilaville, 15 September 1763).

In the meantime, Voltaire had taken up a new task. Soon after his unsuccessful participation in a collective undertaking, he had decided to put into execution a personal project which he had already outlined in 1734, in the *Lettres philosophiques*.[7] On 1 May 1761 he presented his idea to Duclos: "Après le dictionnaire de l'Académie, ouvrage d'autant plus utile que la langue commence à se corrompre, je ne connais point d'entreprise plus digne de l'Académie et plus honorable pour la littérature que celle de donner nos auteurs classiques avec des notes instructives." Voltaire wished to reserve for himself the works of Corneille because "c'est lui qui commença à rendre notre langue respectable chez les étrangers," and suggested that some of his fellow Academicians set to work on other classical authors. He outlined also the principal reasons for undertaking such a work: "Il me paraît que cette entreprise fera quelque honneur à notre siècle et à notre patrie. On verra que nos gens de lettres ne méritaient pas l'outrage

---

[6] Naves, *Voltaire et l'Encyclopédie*, p. 153.
[7] See Chapter II, p. 59.

qu'on leur a fait quand on a osé leur imputer des sentiments peu patriotiques, une philosophie dangereuse et même de l'indifférence pour l'honneur des arts qu'ils cultivent" (Best. 8979). Finally, Voltaire proposed that a list of subscribers be drawn up and that the profits go to make up the dowry of Mlle Corneille.[8]

As soon as Voltaire had received the Academy's approval, he enthusiastically set to work. For over a year, his colleagues at the Academy were assailed with shipments from Ferney. Duclos was the principal target of Voltaire's correspondence, which had become a ceaseless flow of queries, reminders, entreaties and exhortations. The work advanced rapidly, and the list of subscribers, with the King at the head, was impressive. Nevertheless, difficulties and complications soon arose. First of all, the task itself grew larger as it advanced. From the original five or six volumes Voltaire had first planned, the *Commentaire* expanded eventually to twelve. As the work progressed and the burden grew heavier, Voltaire became more and more impatient with Corneille. At first the scope of the work had been modest. In May 1761, he had written to the duc de Nivernais: "Je pense ... qu'il convient de borner nos remarques aux bonnes pièces de Corneille, et d'indiquer seulement les beaux endroits qui se trouvent dans les pièces moins dignes de son génie" (Best. 9011). Then, as he became more thorough in examining Corneille, he lost his tolerance. Three months later he declared to d'Olivet that he saw "des scènes sublimes" in Corneille's, plays, but that he saw also "des tas de barbarismes et de solécismes qui révoltent, et de froids raisonnements alambiqués qui glacent ... enfin vingt pièces entières, dans lesquelles à peine y a-t-il un morceau qui demande grâce pour le reste." He was drawn to make an inevitable comparison and came to the conclusion that: "Dans le siècle passé, il n'y eut que le seul Racine qui écrivit des tragédies avec une pureté et une élégance presque continue" (Best. 9172, 20 August 1761). Voltaire summed up his attitude in a striking

---

[8] Marie-Françoise Corneille was a distant relative of the great Corneille and had been living in poverty until Voltaire heard of her in 1760. He took her in, educated her, and found her a husband. Her presence at Ferney inspired the patriarch to begin his work on Corneille, and although Voltaire indicates in a previous letter to Duclos (Best. 8950), and in another to d'Argental (Best. 8980) that the suggestion had come from the secretary of the Academy, it is evident from the thoroughness of his proposal that the project was indeed his own.

comparison: "Je traite Corneille tantôt comme un Dieu, tantôt comme un cheval de Carosse" (Best. 9191), to d'Argental, 31 August 1761).

Difficulties arose also in his relations with the Academy. While at the outset he had pledged submission, "je me conforme en tout aux ordres que l'Académie voudra bien me faire parvenir par vous" (Best. 8979, to Duclos, 1 May 1761), he soon expressed dissatisfaction with the Company. For one thing, he found it too slow in its performance; he remarked to d'Argental: "J'aurai plutôt achevé tout l'ouvrage que l'académie aura lu trente de mes remarques. Un membre va vite, les corps ont peine à se remuer" (Best. 9151, 9 August 1761). He found also that the Academy's commentaries were sometimes weak: "Quelles pauvres observations, que ses observations sur mes observations concernant Polieucte!" (Best. 9390, to d'Argental, 29 November 1761); often he found them unacceptable: "Elle a beau dire, je ne peux aller contre mon cœur" (Best. 9280, to d'Argental, 11 October 1761). He ended by asserting his independence and declared to his *confrère* Saurin: "Je suis bien aise de recueillir d'abord les sentiments de l'académie, après quoy je dirai hardiment mais modestement la vérité. ... J'admirerai le beau, je distinguerai le médiocre, je noterai le mauvais. Il faudrait être un lâche ou un sot pour écrire autrement" (Best. 9285, 15 October 1761). Even after the work was finished, there was disagreement over the final presentation of the *Commentaire*. The Academy found that the *épître dédicatoire* was not sufficiently respectful. This time, Voltaire complied with the Academy's wishes, and informed his printer: "L'académie veut que son épître dédicatoire soit de la façon que je vous l'envoie. Tous les corps ont leurs formalités, et la plupart ridicules" (Best. 10782, to Cramer, 4 January 1764). The dedication was deferential in tone and informed the public that although the work bore the name of the Academy, any faults it contained were attributable to the author (Moland, XXXI, 177).

As soon as the work appeared in print, it met with unfavorable commentary. One of the more common criticisms consisted in saying that Voltaire had attempted to discredit Corneille in order to elevate his own dramatic achievement. Grimm, a discerning and knowledgeable observer of eighteenth-century France, conceded that Voltaire had been harsh in his critique: "Il est vrai qu'on voit à mesure qu'il continue son travail, que son dégoût augmente, et que son aversion naturelle pour tout ce qui manque de goût et de délicatesse reprend le dessus." Nevertheless, he defended Voltaire's work and offered the following assessment: "Vous trouverez dans ses *Commentaires* une foule de remarques négligemment écrites, faites à la hâte, peu approfondies, quelquefois peu importantes, d'autres fois susceptibles de plus de lumières et d'un plus grand développement; mais je crois qu'aucun esprit équitable n'y trouvera cette envie de déprimer le génie de Corneille, qu'on lui a si indiscrètement et si injustement reprochée." [9] As a friend of the Encyclopedists, and of Diderot in particular, Grimm cannot be accused of wanting to flatter Voltaire by taking his defense. The *Commentaire* had also met with a favorable reaction from Diderot on one occasion. On 3 October 1762, the philosophe informed Sophie Volland that Voltaire had sent him the commentary of *Cinna* and added: "Je n'ai pu m'empêcher de lui dire que cela étoit vrai, juste, intéressant et beau, parce que c'est la vérité; seulement, je lui ai trouvé plus d'indulgence que je n'en aurois eu; il n'a pas repris tout ce qui m'a semblé répréhensible." [10]

In writing the *Commentaire sur Corneille*, Voltaire had been motivated by his attitude towards literature in general and by his interpretation of the Academy's role in particular. The work has to be judged, therefore, in the light of the author's intentions and literary prejudices. It seems clear, first of all, that he never intended to disparage the work of Corneille and that he was sincere in asserting that his *Commentaire* "est un monument que j'ai élevé à la gloire de Corneille et de ma nation" (Best. 9192, to Chennevières, 31 August 1761). He truly admired Corneille in spite of his faults and recognized Corneille's importance and innovative role in the history of literature: "Corneille, malgré tous ses défauts, était sublime et sage dans le temps qu'on ne représentait sur les autres théâtres de l'Europe que des rêves extravagants" (Best. 9694, to Duclos, 7 June 1762). He was severe with the playwright because of his sincere desire to present his contemporaries, both within and outside France, with "une Ecole de grammaire et de poésie" (Best. 9191, to d'Argental, 31 August 1761). The Academy, by patronizing this type of undertaking, was thus going to render a valuable service: "C'est un moyen sûr de fixer la langue, et d'éclairer les doutes des étrangers. On parlera le français plus facilement, grâce aux soins de l'Académie" (Best. 9242, to Ivan Ivanovich Shuvalov, 19 September 1761).

---

[9] Grimm, V, 502.
[10] Diderot, IV, 185.

Furthermore, Voltaire's treatment of Corneille was by no means unique but rather was characteristic of an entire school of thought. Voltaire and his former master d'Olivet were the "représentants du rigorisme puriste le plus absolu," and before Voltaire's *Commentaire* "il y a toute une littérature qui offre l'enseignement de la langue par les bons écrivains." [11] Such undertakings had already been initiated within the Academy as well. Gustave Lanson provides us with the following background history:

> Depuis le commencement du siècle, l'idée de rendre l'Académie "plus utile à l'Etat" travaillait quelques académiciens, l'abbé de St. Pierre, Valincour, Fénelon, etc. On hésita entre "une grammaire" et des "observations sur les bons auteurs." Entre 1700 et 1705, l'Académie examina les ouvrages de Malherbe, Racan, Balzac, Vaugelas, Perrot d'Ablancourt. Elle examina en 1719-1720 le *Quinte Curce* de Vaugelas, et entre 1720-1730 la tragédie d'*Athalie*. En 1738 parurent dans le même esprit les remarques de l'abbé d'Olivet sur Racine. [12]

For Voltaire and for the other *puristes* of eighteenth-century France, the literature of the seventeenth century represented a culminating point in arts. As they were concerned with stemming the apparent decadence of eighteenth-century literature, their principal goal was to "conserver à tout prix et dans toute sa pureté la belle langue qui, sous Louis XIV a été portée au plus haut point de perfection dans tous les genres." [13] Even the best authors of the seventeenth century had not been infallible, however, and their works could be presented as examples only with appropriate corrections or comments. Voltaire was thus typical of the purists who set themselves up as judges with simple logic or "la raison" as their principal guideline: "La raison et l'analogie ne sont abandonnées que dans les cas où l'usage le veut absolument." [14] There was, however, an inherent weakness in the method of the purists: "ils s'érigent en juges de la langue, mais trop souvent

---

[11] Alexis François, *La Grammaire du Purisme et l'Académie française au XVIIIe siècle* (Paris: G. Bellais, 1905), pp. 157 and 95.

[12] Voltaire, *Lettres philosophiques*, II, 182.

[13] Léon Vernier, *Etude sur Voltaire grammairien et la grammaire au XVIIIe siècle* (Paris: Hachette, 1888), p. 83.

[14] Pierre-Joseph Thoulier d'Olivet, *Remarques sur la langue françoise* (Paris: Barbou, 1767), p. 38.

sans autre référence que leur sentiment personnel, leur propre manière d'interpréter la grammaire et l'usage." [15] This was also the principal shortcoming of the *Commentaire sur Corneille*.

For Voltaire, this personal approach represented an essential aspect of the critic's art: "Taste, rather than theory, was for Voltaire the only true basis of literary judgement." [16] As a direct consequence, a judge of literature had to be a writer himself: "Ce n'est pas assez de savoir la langue, il faut connaître le théâtre" (Best. 9290, to d'Alembert, 20 October 1761). This attitude serves to explain the frequently uncompromising stance he adopted in his dealings with the Academy. As he explained to d'Alembert: "Je ne me relâcherai en rien, parce que je suis sûr que j'ai raison; j'en suis sûr, parce que j'ai cinquante ans d'expérience, parce que je me connais au théâtre" (Best. 9772, to d'Alembert, 12 July 1762). It also explains Voltaire's biased approach on even the most basic questions pertaining to the theater, for his conception of the dramatic arts differed greatly from that of Corneille: "His conception of the theatre ... tended to be philosophic rather than moral in the seventeenth-century sense, which tended to be more concerned with the improvement of the individual rather than of society as a whole." [17] Nevertheless, Voltaire's work attracted wide attention and considerable approbation. The *Journal Encyclopédique* rebutted the critics of Voltaire's work and found that,

> les personnes de goût, faisant abstraction et du nom de Corneille et de celui de Voltaire, des tems et des circonstances, n'apperçoivent qu'un homme de génie qui relève les beautés et les défauts des chefs-d'œuvre d'un homme de génie, pour avoir occasion de donner les meilleurs préceptes, et pour développer tous les secrets de son art, pour instruire les Etrangers qui veulent connoitre notre langue, et les jeunes gens qui s'exercent dans la carrière pénible et dangereuse du théâtre. [18]

If nothing else, the *Commentaire* had at least achieved the distinction of being the best known work of its kind: "Le *Commentaire* n'est au

---

[15] François, p. 233.
[16] Williams, p. 144.
[17] *Ibid.*, p. 247.
[18] *Le Journal Encyclopédique*, 1 June 1764, p. 163.

fond que le manifeste d'une école: c'est la grammaire du purisme au dix-huitième siècle." [19]

The publication of the *Commentaire* had also been a huge financial success. Theodore Besterman cites the following facts:

> The edition eventually brought in 100,000 francs for Mlle Corneille's benefit, an enormous figure which was wholly due to Voltaire's business acumen and to his vast prestige and far-flung correspondence, which secured subscriptions for 200-250 copies each from the monarch of Russia, the Empire and France. Voltaire... also bought 100 copies, and the rest of the subscription list reads like a miniature Who's who. [20]

Mlle Corneille's dowry had been amply provided for. In addition, her marriage, which took place in 1763, received an unusual honor. Voltaire had asked and obtained from the Academy the authorization to sign the marriage contract in the name of all its members (Best. 10210, Duclos to Voltaire, 19 February 1763). [21]

On the other hand, Voltaire had failed to achieve what had been one of his principal aims in undertaking this task. He had not succeeded in giving the Academy the impetus to continue with similar works. From the beginning he had urged other Academicians to emulate him: "M. le cardinal de Bernis et m. l'archevêque de Lyon feraient une chose digne de leur esprit et de leurs places de présider à une édition des oraison funèbres et des sermons des illustres Bossuet et Massillon. Les fables de la Fontaine ont besoin de notes, surtout pour l'instruction des étrangers" (Best. 8979, to Duclos, 1 May 1761). Voltaire was hoping to inspire his *confrères* with his own enthusiasm: "Il faut tâcher que tout le monde en soit aussi entousiasmé que moi. Rien ne se fait sans un peu d'entousiasme" (Best. 9191, to d'Argental, 31 August 1761). Instead, he met with scepticism. Bernis expressed the opinion that, "Notre académie ne faira, en corps que des ouvrages médiocres" (Best. 9686, to Voltaire, 4 June 1762). The abbé d'Olivet was equally discouraging. In answer to the query "Quel grand homme prenez vous pour votre part?" (Best. 8951, Voltaire to

---

[19] Vernier, p. 163.
[20] Besterman, *Voltaire*, p. 405.
[21] See also *Registres*, III, p. 171.

d'Olivet, 10 April 1761), the abbé wrote: "Dans votre dernière lettre vous me parlez du Projet de travailler sur nos auteurs classiques. Le secrétaire de la Compagnie en parla samedi pour la première fois, mais en deux mots, et on ne délibéra point là-dessus. Hélas, mon cher, que vous connaissez peu l'Académie d'à présent. Si vous étiez à portée d'y paroître, je doute qu'il vous arrivât de vous y montrer deux fois" (Best. 8961, c. 20 April 1761). [22] As a result of this atmosphere, the *Commentaire sur Corneille* remained the only work of its kind to be published under the auspices of the Academy, and Voltaire's example had failed to bring any concrete results. [23] In 1761, Voltaire had made a comment about his *confrères* which turned out to be an accurate evaluation of the Academy in its later stages as well: "Je souhaite qu'on aille aussi vite que moi, mais les Français parlent vite et agissent lentement, leur vivacité est dans les propositions, et non dans l'action, témoin cent projets que j'ai vûs commencez avec chaleur et abandonnez avec dégoût" (Best. 9158, to d'Argental, 15 October 1761).

After the publication of the *Commentaire* we note a longer period of inactivity in Voltaire's relations with the Academy. This relative calm was momentarily interrupted, as we have seen, by his campaign against the président de Brosses. Voltaire showed a more active interest in the Academy during the last years of his life, a time when the situation inside the Company had stabilized, following the factional disputes between the philosophes and the *dévots*. Voltaire himself had mellowed considerably and had become well-intentioned toward all his colleagues in the Academy. His attitude is well illustrated by the preface of *Don Pèdre,* published in 1775, which elicited the following disapproval of Meister: "La tragédie de Don Pèdre est précédée d'une longue épître dédicatoire à M. d'Alembert, où l'on souffre de

---

[22] The abbé d'Olivet had already become discouraged in 1736; at the time the Academy was working on the third edition of the dictionary, and he had written: "Nos délibérations depuis six mois n'ont servi qu'à faire voir qu'il était impossible que rien de systématique partît d'une compagnie" (Pellisson and d'Olivet, II, 430).

[23] The idea had not been abandoned, however. In 1765, Duclos initiated a collective project on Boileau and later, during the secretaryships of d'Alembert and of Marmontel, commentaries of Molière, La Fontaine, Quinault, and La Bruyère were also begun. Only the Molière was given to a printer for publication, on condition that its provenience be kept secret (François, p. 123).

voir toute la peine que l'auteur s'est donnée pour louer les principaux membres de l'Académie, les premiers aspirants, les dames et les grands qui protègent les lettres, enfin la ville et la cour en gros et en détail." [24] The preface was simply an expression of Voltaire's conciliatory attitude at a time when he had abandoned polemics and was principally interested in gaining the good will of his *confrères*.

A year later, however, the patriarch of Ferney became engaged in a new controversy and sought the backing of the Academy for his cause. As in the case of the *Commentaire sur Corneille*, Voltaire was defending the interests of French literature. Only the nature of the threat was different this time; it was not a vice inherent in French culture, but a danger that came from outside.

In 1776 the first volumes of Le Tourneur's *Shakespeare traduit de l'anglais* were published and immediately set off Voltaire's indignant reaction. He wrote to d'Argental:

> Auriez vous lu deux volumes de ce misérable dans lesquels il veut nous faire regarder Shakespear comme le seul modèle de la véritable Tragédie? Il l'appelle, *le dieu du théâtre*. Il sacrifie tous les Français, sans exception, à son idole, comme on sacrifiait autrefois des cochons à Cérès. Il ne daigne pas même nommer Corneille et Racine; ces deux grands hommes sont seulement enveloppés dans la proscription générale, sans que leurs noms soient prononcés. (Best. 19082, 19 July 1776)

Voltaire then drafted a short treatise attacking le Tourneur and criticizing Shakespeare, and sent it to d'Alembert in order to obtain the Academy's endorsement (Best. 19087). D'Alembert read the work at a meeting of the Academy and reported the following results to Voltaire: "Vos réflexions sur Shakespear nous ont paru si intéressantes pour la littérature en géneral, et pour la littérature française en particulier, si utiles surtout au maintain du bon goût, que nous sommes persuadés que le Public en entendroit la lecture avec la plus grande satisfaction dans la séance du 25 de ce mois, où les prix doivent être distribués." [25] The Academy only requested that Voltaire make a

---

[24] Grimm, XI, 33. Meister had been Grimm's secretary and took over the *Correspondance* in 1773, when Grimm decided to devote himself fully to a diplomatic career.

[25] i.e. 25 August, the day of Saint-Louis.

few changes, as d'Alembert explained: "Vous pourriez, au lieu des grossièretés (inlisibles publiquement) que vous citez de Shakespear, y substituer quelques autres passages ridicules et lisibles qui ne vous manqueront pas" (Best. 19103, 4 August 1776). Because time was short, d'Alembert made the deletions himself and read the modified diatribe to the assembly present on the twenty-fifth of that month. Meister gave an account of the occasion and noted that Voltaire's letter had amused the public and apparently had not offended anyone:

> Nous observons seulement ici, comme une preuve mémorable des dispositions pacifiques qui règnent aujourd'hui entre les nations rivales de l'Europe que cette singulière diatribe fut écoutée patiemment d'un bout à l'autre par un très grand nombre d'Anglais du rang le plus distingué, qui se trouvèrent présents à la séance, et nommément de M. l'ambassadeur, qui se permit même de sourire à tous les traits plaisants dont cet écrit fourmille.[26]

The reading did not please everyone, however. Voltaire had hoped to further authenticate his work by having the official Academy printer publish it, but permission was denied by the King. D'Alembert explained: "On dit que les Dévots de Versailles lui ont persuadé que votre morceau sur Shakespear était injurieux à la religion, quoiqu'on ait retranché soigneusement à la lecture publique tous les passages indécens du Tragique anglois" (Best. 19180, 1 October 1776). Others believed the motives for the suppression to be political: that Louis XVI did not want to give official sanction to a writing that could offend the English.[27] Eventually the ban on the printing was lifted, but according to d'Alembert, the work was still generally considered as "un ouvrage impie" (Best. 19207, to Voltaire, 15 October 1776).

The tone of Voltaire's work could rightly be characterized as offensive, for his critique appears unusually harsh. Also, the comments and accusations appearing in his letters at the time are striking in their violence and evident bias, especially if we compare them to opinions on Shakespeare he had expressed earlier, notably in the eighteenth *lettre philosophique*, "Sur la tragédie." He now came to

---

[26] Grimm, XI, 319.
[27] *Ibid.*, pp. 298 and 319.

regret his earlier writings: "Ce qu'il y a d'affreux, c'est que le monstre a un parti en France; et pour comble de calamité et d'horreur, c'est moi qui le premier montrai aux Français quelques perles que j'avais trouvées dans son énorme fumier. Je ne m'attendais pas que je servirais un jour à fouler aux pieds les couronnes de Racine et de Corneille, pour en orner le front d'un histrion barbare" (Best. 19082, to d'Argental, 19 July 1776). Actually, Voltaire's basic attitude towards Shakespeare had not really changed.[28] He still held the convictions expressed in the *Lettres philosophiques* which we find summarized in a letter to Horace Walpole, written in 1768. Speaking of Shakespeare, he found that: "C'est une belle nature, mais sauvage; nulle régularité, nulle bienséance, nul art; de la bassesse avec de la grandeur; de la bouffonerie avec du terrible; c'est le chaos de la Tragédie dans lequel il y a cent traits de lumière" (Best. 14179). In judging Shakespeare with the standards applicable to classical theater, "Voltaire was merely reflecting the critical limitations of his age."[29]

Voltaire's language in 1776 was simply distorted by the heat of a polemical intent. He was defending the great traditions of French dramatic art in the face of this foreign incursion: "Ma principale intention et le vrai but de mon travail sont que tout le public soit bien instruit de tout l'excès de la turpitude infâme qu'on ose opposer à la majesté de notre théâtre" (Best. 19119, to La Harpe, 15 August 1776). The public interest in Shakespeare was all the more irritating at a time when his own plays represented and emulated the literary glories of a bygone era. He complained to d'Argental: "Le Kain ... me dit que presque toute la jeunesse de Paris est pour le Tourneur, que les échafauds et les bordels anglais l'emportent sur le théâtre de Racine et sur les belles scènes de Corneille, qu'il n'y a plus rien de grand et de décent à Paris que les Gilles de Londres.... J'ai vu finir le règne de la raison et du goût. Je vais mourir en laissant la France barbare" (Best. 19094, 30 July 1776). In the light of these considerations, Voltaire's attack acquires a different meaning, modified by the understanding that "to a large measure Voltaire did not criticize Shakespearean drama per se, but only Shakespeare as the

---

[28] Williams, p. 341. See also Theodore Besterman, *Voltaire on Shakespeare*, Studies on Voltaire and the Eighteenth Century, LIV (Geneva: Institut et Musée Voltaire, 1967).

[29] Williams, p. 321.

symbol of all that was undesirable and unacceptable to French traditions of aesthetic practice." [30]

As was to be expected, Voltaire's attack elicited responses from partisans of Shakespeare. An Irishman, the chevalier Rutlidge, published his *Observations à Messieurs de l'Académie française au sujet d'une lettre de m. de Voltaire* in 1776, an Italian, Baretti, wrote a *Discours sur Shakespeare et sur M. de Voltaire* in 1777, and an *Apologie de Shakespeare en réponse à la critique de M. de Voltaire*, by the Englishwoman Elizabeth Montagu also appeared in 1777. [31] The following year Voltaire found it necessary to answer the arguments of Mrs. Montagu, and included his reply in the preface to his latest play, *Irène*. The preface was addressed to the Academy: Voltaire was reminding the Company once more of its responsibilities and was hoping to inspire the distinguished Society with some of the zeal he himself had so often exhibited in defending the renown of French arts.

In 1777, Voltaire decided again to participate in the Academy's activities, but in a rather curious and unusual fashion this time. He entered the Academy's regular poetry contest, which had as subject the translation in verse of a passage from the *Iliad*. [32] Voltaire sent in his entry under the name of the marquis de Villette, who subsequently revealed the secret to La Harpe. The latter, who is our principal source for the anecdote, tells us that Voltaire's effort did no better than receive fifth place in the competition, and that the work "n'aurait pas même obtenu une mention si je n'avais, en opinant, ramené mes confrères à mon avis." [33] Although La Harpe attributes Voltaire's whim to an "étrange avidité de gloire," we are more inclined to believe that the project was undertaken for the old poet's own amusement and for the pleasure of mystifying his colleagues.

The year 1778 finally gave Voltaire the long awaited opportunity to attend the meetings of the Academy and to inspire the Company in person. In February, after an absence of thirty years, Voltaire returned to Paris. The visit had taken everyone by surprise, and the

---

[30] *Ibid.*, p. 339.
[31] Mrs. Montagu's work was a translation of an earlier English version published in 1766 in London.
[32] Voltaire's work is found in Moland X, 613-621.
[33] Jean-François La Harpe, *Correspondance littéraire* (Paris: Migneret, 1804-1807), II, 273.

Academy recorded the following minutes for its session of the twelfth: "M^r le Secretaire ... a proposé à la Compagnie de féliciter sur cette arrivée, par une députation extraordinaire et solennelle, un homme si célèbre dans les lettres et si prétieux à l'Académie et à la nation. La Compagnie d'une voix unanime et par acclamation a applaudi à la proposition de M^r le Secretaire" (Registres, III, 423). The enthusiasm of the Academy had not been as unanimous as d'Alembert's minutes would lead us to believe. The memoirs of Bachaumont report that the *dévots* were "scandalisés de la députation de cette compagnie vers le coryphée de l'impiété, en ce qu'indépendamment de l'éclat que faisoit cet acte solennel, il lioit en quelque sorte le clergé aux hommages qu'on lui rendoit en la personne de plusieurs cardinaux, archevêques, évêques et abbés, membres de l'académie, et par conséquent censés avoir adhéré à la délibération." [34] Nevertheless, in spite of any efforts on the part of the clerical party to spoil Voltaire's triumph, the Academy continued honoring its most illustrious member with special distinctions. The tide of public sentiment was too overwhelming in Paris, and swept aside any obstacles set up by Voltaire's detractors. Meister reported that "l'orgueil encyclopédique a paru diminué de moitié, la Sorbonne a frémi, le Parlament a gardé le silence, toute la littérature s'est émue, tout Paris s'est empressé de voler aux pieds de l'idole." [35]

On 26 February the Academy was informed by its secretary that Voltaire was seriously ill and decided to send a delegation to visit the patriarch. On 2 March, Voltaire's condition was still critical, and the Academy recorded: "L'Académie a député une seconde fois Mrs de St Lambert et de La Harpe pour s'informer de l'état de Mr de Voltaire et elle a arrêté qu'on y enverroit désormais à chaque séance" (Registres, III, 426). On 19 March, d'Alembert read the "Epître dédicatoire" of *Irène* to the meeting of the Academy. After the session, a delegation visited Voltaire in order to congratulate him on the success of his new play and to thank him for the dedication (Registres, III, 427). Following each of the visits, a report was made to the Academy and Voltaire's comments and expressions of gratitude dutifully recorded in the minutes (Registres, III, 423-428).

---

[34] Bachaumont, XI, 127.
[35] Grimm, XII, 53.

Finally, on 30 March, the patriarch was well enough to appear in person at a meeting of the Academy. The minutes for this memorable day read as follows: "Mr de Voltaire est venu à l'Académie sur les quatre heures. M^r le Directeur et tous les Académiciens présents ont été au devant de lui dans la première salle. Il est entré dans la salle d'assemblée, et M^r le Directeur l'a prié de prendre la première place, et de présider à la séance, ce qu'il a accepté par déférence pour la Compagnie" (Registres, III, 429). The Academicians present at the meeting were: Arnaud, Paulmy, Voltaire, d'Alembert, Marmontel, Gaillard, Watelet, Thomas, Saurin, Beauzée, Millot, La Harpe, Saint-Lambert, Chastellux, Duras, Beauvau, Foncemagne, Sainte-Palaye, Bréquigny, Suard, Boismont. Members of the clergy were conspicuously absent that day. Meister notes that the reception was an honor that the Academy "n'avait jamais fait à aucun de ses membres, pas même aux princes étrangers qui ont daigné assister à ses assemblées." [36] The members of the Academy further distinguished Voltaire by making him Director for the new quarter. It was again a notable distinction, for the Director was always chosen by lot. The patriarch then listened to a reading by d'Alembert because, as the minutes explain, "quelque désir que l'Académie eût de l'entendre, elle a craint qu'il ne se fatiguât trop à parler, et elle a invité M^r le Secretaire à lire l'*Eloge de Despréaux*" (Registres, III, 430). For d'Alembert, this was yet another occasion to pay tribute to the patriarch, and the eulogy of Boileau was a skillful panegyric of Voltaire as well. At the end of this relatively short meeting, the assembly escorted Voltaire out, and the old philosophe left it "en lui réitérant avec les expressions les plus vives tous ses remerciements" (Registres, III, 430).

Voltaire attended the Academy's meetings again on 6 and 27 April and on 4 and 7 May. In the meantime, the Company continued favoring him with conspicuous marks of respect. On 9 April it decreed that "toutes les fois que Mr de Voltaire viendroit à la séance, après l'heure sonnée, il auroit son droit de présence, et que les Académiciens arrivez avant lui recevroient le même droit, mais non ceux qui arriveroient après" (Registres, III, 431). On 25 April the Academy recorded: "Un particulier ayant envoyé de Bâle à l'Académie un ouvrage où Mr de Voltaire est grossièrement insulté, la Compagnie a chargé

---

[36] *Ibid.*, p. 68.

Mᵣ le Secretaire de renvoyer ce livre à l'auteur, et de lui dire qu'elle ne reçoit de satyres contre personne, et encore moins contre un homme aussi cher et aussi respectable pour elle que Mᵣ de Voltaire" (Registres, III, 431).

While he was flattered by these marks of consideration and probably enjoyed the ceremonial atmosphere that marked his appearance at the Academy, Voltaire soon showed a desire to make the meetings of the Company more productive. His spirit and energy were remarkable for a man eighty-four years old, and before coming to the Academy, he informed d'Alembert: "Tout mort que je suis je compte venir aujourd'hui à l'Académie. Je tâcherai de bien voir, de faire bien voir et de commencer dès demain à travailler sans discontinuer. Je veux mourir en m'éclairant avec vous et en vous servant" (Best. 19963, 30 March 1778). His intention "de faire bien voir" materialized a month later into a lengthy proposal submitted to the meeting of 7 May and recorded as follows:

> Il a été résolu, sur la proposition de Mr de Voltaire, qu'on travailleroit sans délai à un nouveau Dictionnaire qui contiendra:
> L'Etimologie reconnue de chaque mot, et quelquefois l'Etimologie probable.
> La conjugaison des verbes irréguliers qui sont peu en usage.
> Les diverses acceptions de chaque terme avec les exemples tirés des auteurs les plus approuvés.
> Toutes les expressions pittoresques, et énergiques de Montagne, d'Amiot, de Charron, etc. qu'il est à souhaiter qu'on fasse revivre, et dont nos voisins se sont saisis.
> En ne s'appesantissant pas sur aucun de ces objets, mais en les traitant tous, on peut faire un ouvrage aussi agréable que nécessaire, ce seroit à la fois une grammaire, une rhétorique, une poétique, sans l'ambition d'y prétendre. Chaque Académicien peut se charger d'une lettre de l'alphabet; l'Académie examinera le travail de chacun de ses membres. Elle y fera les changemens, les additions et les retranchements convenables. (Registres, III, 432)

The same day, Voltaire wrote to Wagnière and asked his secretary to send him "tout ce qui regarde la langue française" from his library at Ferney (Best. 20010). The patriarch was seriously preparing himself for the task at hand. The undertaking promised to be especially arduous, as most of Voltaire's colleagues lacked not only the competency but even the dedication necessary for carrying out the project. On 8 March Mme Denis informed Wagnière: "Mon oncle se porte bien, il va à l'académie et il y crie comme un diable. Il veut leur faire faire un nouveau Dictionnaire. Ces Messieurs rechignent, ils craignent que cela ne leur donne trop de peine" (Best. 20011). Voltaire was well aware of the reluctance shared by his fellow Academicians, but was determined to overcome the Company's inertness. Voltaire's doctor, Tronchin, reported his patient as saying, "ce sont des fainéants... accoutumés à croupir dans l'oisiveté. Mais je les ferai bien marcher." [37]

In his enthusiasm, Voltaire failed to consider the rapidly deteriorating state of his health, and this new and demanding activity was one of the contributing factors that brought on his death a few weeks later. Tronchin noted in his letter that Voltaire's work on the dictionary had been the principal cause of his death. [38] Meister provided a similar explanation:

> Ayant appris qu'à une séance de l'Académie, à laquelle il ne put assister, le projet qu'il avait fait adopter à ces messieurs pour une nouvelle édition de leur Dictionnaire avait essuyé des contradictions sans nombre, il craignit de le voir abandonné, et voulut composer un discours pour les faire revenir à son premier plan. Pour remonter ses nerfs affaiblis, il prit une quantité prodigieuse de café; cet excès dans son état, et un travail suivi de dix ou douze heures, renouvelèrent toutes ses souffrances, et le jetèrent dans un accablement affreux. [39]

Voltaire had thus fulfilled the letter of the promise made to d'Alembert: "Je veux mourir... en vous servant" (Best. 19963).

On 1 June 1778 the minutes of the Academy read: L'Académie a appris avec la plus vive douleur la mort de Mr de Voltaire, décédé le samedi 30 Mai à onze heures du soir" (Registres, III, 434). The Academy's principal concern now became the commemoration of its deceased member and the dictionary was willingly abandoned, since the Company recognized itself incapable of carrying out the task

---

[37] Desnoiresterres, VIII, 365.
[38] *Ibid.*
[39] Grimm, XII, 108.

without the initiator of the project. This impotence, or this unwillingness, is clearly expressed in the minutes of the meeting held on 25 May, when the Academy had approved Voltaire's proposal:

> On a délibéré ensuite sur la manière de procéder au travail nécessaire pour les additions proposées, et les avis s'étant trouvés partagés, on a arrêté qu'attendu la maladie de Mr le Directeur, et l'absence d'un grand nombre d'Académiciens, on remettrait le partage du travail au temps où Mr le Directeur pourroit venir à l'Académie, et qu'on le prieroit alors de se charger de quelque article du nouveau Dictionnaire, pour juger d'après cet article, et après l'avoir examiné, quelle seroit la meilleure forme à donner à ce nouveau Dictionnaire. (Registres, III, 434)

It is highly unlikely that anything would have been accomplished on the project, even if Voltaire had lived longer. The patriarch had failed to correctly estimate the Academy's potential by misunderstanding the true nature of the Company. By 1778, the Academy was enjoying more prestige than ever before. Its fame had attracted the most distinguished visitors from the courts of Europe [40] and its public assemblies gathered the most brilliant society of Paris. Its functions, however, were more social than literary and it was beginning to incur a growing number of criticisms for this reason. Mme Du Deffand wrote to Voltaire in 1769: "Vous avez beau dire, Monsieur, vous ne me persuaderez jamais, que ce qui produit de si mauvais ouvrages, et qui introduit un si détestable goût soit un établissement bon et utile; pourquoy inciter les gens à parler quand ils n'ont rien à dire?" (Best. 14927). The philosophes were partly to blame, because, as we have seen, they were more interested in acquiring adherents to their party than in recruiting Academiciens possessing literary talent. Thus, Collé remarked in 1771: "Il est incroyable que l'Académie s'associe des gens ignorés, tandis qu'elle ne songe pas à des gens de lettres célèbres dans l'Europe savante par leurs ouvrages." [41]

The reasons behind the Academy's shortcomings as a literary body were more complex, however. The Academy's deficiencies were closely

---

[40] In 1766, the *prince héréditaire de Brunswick* had visited the Academy; in 1768 Christian VII, King of Denmark; in 1771 Gustavus III, King of Sweden, and in 1777 Emperor Joseph II.

[41] Collé, III, 312.

linked with the very nature of the body and it was perhaps necessary to have the more objective eye of a foreigner in order to analyze this reality perceptively. Meister quoted the following rationalization from an anonymous discourse that circulated in 1777:

> Plaignons l'Académie de ne pouvoir admettre d'ouvrages d'un ton plus mâle et plus hardi! Telle est sa constitution, telles sont les chaînes dont Richelieu l'investit à sa naissance. Eh! qui sait si cet adroit tyran ne calcula pas, en la créant, que cette institution mettait à jamais la plus grande partie des gens de lettres sous la discipline du gouvernement; que, dès ce moment, jaloux de parvenir aux places qu'elle offrait, et ensuite jouir en paix du frivole honneur d'y être assis, il ne sortirait plus de leur plume rien de grand, rien de fort, rien de libre? [42]

D'Alembert himself seems to have held the opinion that it was hopeless to expect any worthwhile productions from the Academy. In his *Histoire des membres de l'Académie* he speaks of the "timidité des compagnies, qui, toujours en garde pour ne point se compromettre, n'osent prononcer affirmativement sur des questions qu'un particulier déciderait sans hésiter. Elles craignent que le plus léger changement dans leurs principes, leurs opinions, leurs usages, n'entraîne des inconvénients; et pour éviter ces prétendus inconvénients elles laissent subsister les erreurs et les abus." [43] Voltaire, perhaps because of his prolonged absence from the Academy's meetings, had never perceived this reality. He had, of course, always been critical of the Academy's membership and hoped to see the day "quand l'Académie aura dégorgé les prêtres qui l'ont pestiférée" (Best. 19683, to Marmontel, 10 October 1777). He had also condemned the Academy's more frivolous activities. Thus, in 1777, when the Academy's principal concern was with a fashionable quarrel over two musicians, when the Company itself had become divided into two factions, the "Gluckistes" and the "Piccinistes," [44] Voltaire wrote to La Harpe: "Nous avons un extrême

---

[42] Grimm, XI, 506.

[43] Jean Lerond d'Alembert, *Œuvres de d'Alembert* (1821 rpt. Geneva: Slatkine, 1967), II, 474.

[44] Gluck, a German composer, and Piccinni, an Italian, had recently acquired great popularity in France, and represented two sharply different approaches to music. Each musician had a group of zealous fans who defended the tastes of their respective composer.

besoin de vous pour ne pas devenir des barbares subsistant uniquement de musique italienne et allemande" (Best. 19674, 6 October 1777). He thought also that the Academicians' time could be generally spent in a more productive manner and occasionally offered suggestions to d'Alembert:

> Croyez vous que ce fût aussi le temps de donner, pour sujet des prix, non des éloges, dans lesquels il y a toujours de la déclamation, de l'exagération, et qui par là ne passeront jamais à la postérité, mais des discours tels que vous en savez faire, des jugements sur les grands hommes, à la manière de Plutarque? Rien ne serait, ce me semble, plus instructif, rien ne formerait plus le jugement et le goût de nos jeunes écrivains. (Best. 18241, 26 February 1775)

Yet, in general, Voltaire had faith in the Academy and found that it represented considerable improvement over previous ages. The often ridiculed discourses presented to the eloquence contests of the Academy were to him the best proof of this advance: "J'avoue que nos discours pour l'académie du temps de Louis XIV n'approchaient pas de ceux qu'on fait aujourd'hui; c'est l'effet de la vraie philosophie; elle a donné plus de vérité à nos esprits" (Best. 18541, to comte de Schomberg, 19 September 1775). The best indication of his confidence is furnished by his actions during the Corneille enterprise and the Shakespeare controversy. On both occasions, he considered it most important to obtain the endorsement of the Academy. In 1761, he wrote to d'Olivet: "Vous sentez qu'il est important qu'un tel ouvrage ait la sanction du corps" (Best. 9166). In 1776, speaking of his work on Shakespeare, he remarked: "Je ne dois le faire imprimer qu'en cas que l'Académie y donne une approbation un peu authentique" (Best. 19094, to d'Argental).

Finally, in 1778, his project for the *Dictionnaire historique* became yet another affirmation of his confidence in the Academy's potential. The plan had been submitted with the conviction that the Company had sufficient talent, cohesion and dedication to complete this rather formidable task. Voltaire was spared a disappointment by an untimely death, as the Academy was spared a dilemma, possibly an open conflict, over the issue of its meaning. It had been freed from a burdensome ascendancy and was allowed to resume its usual occupations, its social and ceremonial functions. Moreover, with the death of Voltaire these functions acquired an unprecedented significance. The Company was to devote itself to Voltaire as it had never done before, and after thirty two years of misunderstandings and conflicts, Voltaire was to acquire an importance he had never had in the Academy. He was no longer there to divert the Company from the role it had found for itself, from its function as a decorative symbol.

Chapter V

THE ACADEMY'S TRIBUTE

In a letter to Frederick II written one month after Voltaire's death, d'Alembert reminisced about the patriarch's fateful trip to Paris: "Quand j'appris qu'il avoit formé presque subitement le dessein de venir à Paris, et qu'il étoit déjà en route, j'en fus très affligé, ne doutant pas qu'il ne vînt y chercher la persécution et la mort." [1] D'Alembert's premonition had been wrong in only one detail: persecution came after death. While Voltaire was alive, the popular enthusiasm that celebrated his stay in Paris kept the government's and the Church's malevolence at bay. Once he was dead, he had to deal with the spiritual authorities of the land, and "toutes les sottises qui ont été faites et dites à cette occasion" [2] make up, in the story of Voltaire's life, an odd chapter which partakes of the burlesque as well as of the macabre, and inspires both compassion and scorn. [3]

As was to be expected, the principal conflict arose over the question of funeral rites. Beaumont, the archbishop of Paris, had forbidden a Christian burial. After trying in vain to lift the interdiction, Voltaire's nephews, the abbé Mignot and d'Hornoy, resorted to a subterfuge. Having quietly smuggled Voltaire's body out of Paris, they had it buried with all due ceremony at the abbey of Scellières, in Champagne, where Mignot was the *abbé commendataire*. The bishop of Troyes had received a directive from Paris forbidding the inhumation,

---

[1] Frédéric II, *Œuvres posthumes* (Berlin: Voss and Decker, 1788), XV, 102.
[2] *Ibid.*, p. 78.
[3] For a full and detailed account of the events that followed Voltaire's death, see Desnoiresterres, VIII, 389-526.

but acted too late to prevent it. Only the fear of causing an irreparable scandal kept the more fanatical members of the clergy from carrying out plans for a disinterment. In view of these developments, the government thought it wise to intervene. In order not to aggravate an already tense situation, it prohibited the press from mentioning the name of Voltaire and the *Comédie française* from staging any of his plays for a period of one month.

The Academy was very much involved in these events and found itself in a difficult situation. It was traditional for the Academy to commemorate the passing of one of its members with a service in the church of the Cordeliers, in Paris. On 4 June, d'Alembert informed the Academicians present at the regular meeting that the archbishop of Paris had forbidden the Cordeliers to hold the service, and on 6 June, "M^r le Secrétaire a dit que les Cordeliers lui avoient écrit qu'ils ne pouvoient procéder au service avant que l'Académie eût obtenu l'agrément des puissances civiles et ecclésiastiques" (Registres, III, 435). On 11 June, one of the more influential members of the Academy, the Prince de Rohan, was consulted on the matter: "L'avis de Mr le Prince Louis avoit été d'attendre quelques temps pour faire de nouvelles démarches" (Registres, III, 436). A delegation to Maurepas also failed to get any concrete promises, but the minister, "sans rien promettre de positif, a paru disposé à s'y prêter quand la première fermentation seroit passée." [4]

The Company was willing to be patient, until an event forced it to resolve the question once and for all. More than a year later, on 4 November 1779, it learned that Foncemagne had died, and "avant de procéder au service de feu M. de Foncemagne, il étoit nécessaire que l'Académie prît un parti au sujet de celui de M. de Voltaire" (Registres, III, 460). This time, d'Alembert hoped to circumvent the difficulty by a clever stratagem which was approved by all Academicians present at the meeting of 11 November: "Il a été unanimement arrêté que M. le Cardinal de Rohan, grand aumonier, et à ce titre maître de la Chapelle du Louvre, seroit prié par la Compagnie d'obtenir l'agrément du Roi pour que les services funéraires des Académiciens se fissent désormais dans cette chapelle, et pour qu'on célébrât à la fois ceux de Mrs de Voltaire et de Foncemagne" (Registres, III,

---

[4] Bachaumont, XII, 67.

460). The cardinal offered no objections, but asked the Academy for a short delay before giving a definite answer. The Company waited until 16 December, when it heard from Rohan that "il croyait plus convenable pour l'Académie et pour lui que le premier service qui se feroit pour les Académiciens morts fût célébré dans une Eglise de Paris différente de la Chapelle du Louvre" (Registres, III, 462-463). The problem remained intact. A majority of the members then voted to dispense with the particular services altogether, and instead, to hold a general service at the beginning or end of each year. Two days later, the King made it known that "son intention étoit que la Compagnie suivît ses anciens usages" (Registres, III, 463). The Cordeliers were thereupon again notified. The answer was brief: the Père Gardien of the convent informed the Academy on 20 December 1779 that he persevered "dans les mêmes sentiments qu'il a eu l'honneur de manifester à Mr d'Alembert" (Registres, III, 463). D'Alembert proposed to postpone further deliberations on the subject, but it was probably clear to most of those present that the question, in reality, had been settled. Later, in recounting these events, Condorcet observed that the archbishop of Paris "servit malgré lui à détruire une superstition ridicule" (Moland, I, 280).

A contemporary witness to these negotiations remarked that "les partisans de M. de Voltaire ne perdent point de vue sa gloire et cherchent tous les moyens de réparer par de nouveaux triomphes l'insulte que les prêtres lui ont faite." [5] It was evident that "la joie bête et ridicule de tous les fanatiques au sujet de cette mort" [6] only served to reinforce the desire of d'Alembert and of the other Academicians to mark the loss of their mentor in a most ostentatious manner. Similarly, they were liberal in expressing their gratitude to anyone outside the Academy who contributed to the glorification of Voltaire. On 4 June 1778, when Mme Denis gave the Academy a portrait of Voltaire painted by Largillière in 1718 (which the patriarch himself had been promising his *confrères* for more than twenty years), "la Compagnie a reçu ce portrait avec reconnoissance et avec douleur" (Registres, III, 435). The Academy decided the same day "qu'elle ferait faire un second portrait de Mr de Voltaire d'après le buste fait par Mr Houdon

---

[5] *Ibid.*, XIV, 50.

[6] Frédéric II, XV, 79. The quote is from d'Alembert's letter of 29 June to the King of Prussia.

en 1778, et que ces deux portraits faits à 60 ans l'un de l'autre, seroient tous deux placés dans la salle de l'Académie" (Registres, III, 435). The sculptor Houdon gave permission to copy his artwork, and even sent plaster copies of the famous bust to individual Academicians. For his gesture, the artist received a handsome reward from the Company:

> Elle a arrêté que Mr le Secretaire lui enverroit, au nom de l'Académie, une bourse de cent jettons, brodée avec la devise de l'Académie, et de plus un exemplaire relié du Dictionnaire, sur le dos duquel il seroit écrit "donné par l'Académie à Mr Houdon." Elle a encore arrêté qu'indépendamment des deux billets d'entrée qu'il auroit pour chaque séance publique ... il auroit à toutes ces séances ses entrées personnelles sans aucun billet. (Registres, III, 447).

A bust in clay of Voltaire found its way into the assembly hall as well.[7] It had been a gift from d'Alembert and was prominently displayed on the day of St. Louis in 1778.

The St. Louis Day celebrations that year had another surprise for the public: "Mr le Directeur annonça que le sujet du prix de poësie, remis à l'année prochaine, seroit 'un ouvrage en vers à la louange de Mr de Voltaire'" (Registres, III, 441). Furthermore, the poetry prize had been augmented from 500 to 1100 *livres* by an anonymous donation. It was soon public knowledge that both the contribution and the idea for the topic had come from d'Alembert. The proposal had already been made on 3 August, when the Academy had granted and recorded the following request: "Attaché, Messieurs, pendant plus de trente années à feu Mr de Voltaire par l'amitié la plus tendre, connoissant d'ailleurs toute l'admiration dont vous étiez pénetrez pour lui, et dont vous lui avez donné tant de preuves, je crois satisfaire à la fois et vos sentiments et les miens, en vous proposant de donner son Eloge pour sujet du prix de Poésie de l'année prochaine." D'Alembert pointed out, in addition, that one of his principal

---

[7] According to Meister, Mme Denis had also promised to give the Academy a statue of Voltaire but she angered the Academicians by getting married when hardly a year had elapsed after Voltaire's death. D'Alembert and a few other Immortals viewed the marriage "comme une espèce d'adultère spirituel" and stopped seeing the lady. Mme Denis was offended and bequeathed the statue instead to the *Comédie française* (Grimm, XII, 304).

motives for proposing the *Eloge* was "la crainte... de voir quelque autre Académie nous enlever un si beau sujet" (Registres, III, 439). It was decided to keep these deliberations a secret until the day of St. Louis, in order to make the announcement more striking, and also for a very practical reason; La Harpe explains: "Si la chose eût transpiré, il était possible qu'on nous défendît de l'effectuer; mais le programme une fois donné au public, c'eût été un trop grand éclat que de la révoquer, et d'obliger l'académie à choisir un autre sujet." [8] The precaution had apparently not been taken unnecessarily; a few days after the St. Louis day announcement, the *curés* of Paris considered presenting a petition to the King asking him "de vouloir bien interdire à l'Académie française le choix d'un sujet aussi profane, aussi scandaleux que l'éloge de M. de Voltaire." [9] Not every priest was convinced of the desirability of this action, and the petition never materialized; the success of the St. Louis Day commemoration had been too resounding.

The day owed this success mainly to d'Alembert. He had prepared the occasion and helped conduct it with one theme in mind: the glorification of Voltaire. The high point of the afternoon was d'Alembert's reading of his *Eloge de Crébillon* which was "en grande partie l'éloge de Voltaire." [10] The discourse transported the audience, and when d'Alembert reached the final passage, "il s'est en même temps retourné vers le buste, le mouchoir à la main et les larmes aux yeux, et l'enthousiasme général, qui s'étoit déjà manifesté à l'annonce du prix, et toutes les fois qu'on avoit nommé monsieur de Voltaire, a redoublé, et tout le monde a battu des mains, pleuré, sangloté." [11] It was to be expected that this demonstrative tribute to Voltaire would attract a variety of criticisms: "Les gens du monde ont trouvé dans la conduite de M. d'Alembert un peu de faste encyclopédique et peut-être même un peu de maladresse; nos dévots l'ont regardée comme un acte public d'idolâtrie et d'impiété." [12] Detractors soon realized, however, that their efforts were futile in the emotional climate brought on by Voltaire's death, not only in Paris, but in cities beyond the French

---

[8] La Harpe, II, 282.
[9] Grimm, XII, 160.
[10] La Harpe, II, 282
[11] Bachaumont, XII, 90.
[12] Grimm, XII, 159.

borders as well. Towards the end of the year, Paris saw the publication of an *Eloge de Voltaire, lu à l'Académie des sciences et belles-lettres de Berlin, dans une assemblée publique extraordinairement convoquée pour cet objet, le 26 november 1778.* The author was the King of Prussia himself, and Meister found it "beau de voir le grand Frédérick au milieu du tumulte des armes consacrer quelques unes de ses veillées à la mémoire du grand Voltaire." [13] The prestige of the author's name was a considerable boost to d'Alembert's cause, and although it was perhaps an exaggeration to describe the *Eloge* as "un témoignage... qui s'élèvera dans tous les siècles contre les persécuteurs de la philosophie et du génie," [14] its effect at the time probably helped to stifle any budding persecutions.

While honoring the memory of its illustrious member, the Academy had postponed the settlement of an all-important question: that of filling the vacant chair. The delay was understandable, since the seat that had to be filled was not simply chair number twelve of the French Academy, it was the chair of Voltaire. On 1 July 1778, d'Alembert described the situation to Frederick II: "Tous les gens de lettres lui rendent cette justice que personne n'ose se présenter encore pour lui succéder; et il y a tout lieu de croire que l'élection ne se fera pas sitôt. Elle devroit ne se faire jamais, et mon avis, s'il étoit suivi, seroit de laisser la place vacante." [15] Nevertheless, the election did finally take place, and on 28 December 1778 the dramatic author Ducis was chosen to succeed Voltaire. The choice of the Academy was in one sense ironic: Ducis owed a part of his dramatic fame to some adaptations of Shakespeare.

The inauguration of the new Academician took place on 4 March 1779 and Meister reported that "jamais assemblée publique de l'Académie n'avait attiré une affluence de monde aussi prodigieuse; il n'y avait pas un coin de la salle où l'on ne fût plus pressé qu'on ne l'est au parterre de la Comédie le jour d'une première représentation. Les portes, malgré la garde, furent forcées deux ou trois fois, et l'on fut obligé de tirer de la foule plusieurs personnes qui coururent le risque d'y être étouffées." [16] In analyzing the motives that had attracted the

---

[13] *Ibid.*, p. 208.
[14] *Ibid.*, p. 209.
[15] Frédéric II, XV, 95.
[16] Grimm, XII, 228.

public in such numbers to the Academy, La Harpe noted that "il entrait un peu de malignité dans cette curiosité du public.... On ne voulait pas seulement voir comment le récipiendaire se tirerait de l'éloge de son prédécesseur, mais aussi comment notre directeur, l'abbé de Radonvilliers, prêtre et dévot, louerait M. de Voltaire." [17] The abbé had caused a number of his fellow Academicians to worry before the inauguration. On 16 August 1778, d'Alembert had expressed his concern to Frederick II: "Ce qu'il y a de fâcheux, c'est que le successeur de Voltaire sera reçu par un prêtre." His consolation was that "ses confrères supléeront de leur mieux à ce que ce capelan ne dira pas." Attempts had even been made to dissuade Radonvilliers from fulfilling his functions, but the priest had not given up his privilege. [18]

The session opened with the discourse of Ducis, who began: "Il est des grans hommes à qui l'on succède et que personne ne remplace." [19] The speech was a complete success, although its grandiloquence had Meister characterize it as "cette espèce d'éloquence que M. de Voltaire osait appeler du *galithomas*." [20] Voltaire's witticism was appropriate in this instance, since everyone suspected Ducis's friend, Thomas, of having written the discourse, "soupçon qui a paru d'autant plus probable, que jamais Ducis n'avait écrit une ligne de prose." [21] Thus, while the public was enthusiastically applauding the more brilliant passages, Meister heard members of the audience whispering: "Optime, Thomas! optime!" [22]

The discourse of the abbé de Radonvilliers did not fare as well. The abbé, who apparently was an honest man, began by excusing himself for performing a task for which he was ill-suited. He then expressed the hope that Voltaire's works would someday be expurgated of all the passages offensive to religion and to morals, and the rest of the speech disappeared in an unending clamor. Subsequently, when the speech was published, the readers, who had hooted him at the reception of Ducis, realized they had been unfair to the poor abbé. The eulogy turned

---

[17] La Harpe, II, 342.
[18] Frédéric II, XV, 107.
[19] *Choix de discours de réception à l'Académie française* (Paris: Demonville, 1808), II, 166.
[20] Grimm, XII, 229.
[21] La Harpe, II, 342.
[22] Grimm, XII, 229.

out to be "sensée et raisonnable," [23] and was in general highly favorable to Voltaire, characterizing him as a writer who "tenait dans le siècle de Louis XV, la place des beaux génies qui ont illustré le siècle de Louis XIV." [24] The day would not have been complete without a panegyric by d'Alembert, and after a poetry reading by Marmontel, the assembly heard the geometer's tribute to Voltaire. The Academy had recently acquired a bust of Molière by Houdon; considering the two busts decorating the assembly hall, d'Alembert drew a parallel between the seventeenth-century genius and the writer the Academy was commemorating. There was one similarity which d'Alembert had wanted to bring out in particular, as he explained to Frederick II: "J'ai voulu indiquer, mais à mots couverts, et qui ont été bien entendus par l'auditoire, le refus qu'on a fait à Voltaire et à Molière de les enterrer l'un et l'autre dans ce que nous appelons *terre sainte*." [25] The session closed with a reading of "des vers adressés aux mânes de Voltaire." The entire program of the afternoon had thus been devoted to the memory of Voltaire, and "ce plan, dont le public a été très-satisfait, devait être celui de l'académie." [26]

D'Alembert had reason to be gratified with the success of the Academy's commemoration of his late mentor and friend. Still, the ceremonies honoring Voltaire at the Academy had not, in his opinion, sufficiently vexed the *dévots* in France. The Church's attitude regarding the mortal remains of Voltaire remained a matter of great irritation with the geometer. His wish now was to humiliate the French Church in its intransigent attitude by having a commemorative service held outside of France. On 29 February 1780, d'Alembert outlined his purpose to Frederick II: "J'oserois vous proposer, Sire, une petite réparation qui mortifieroit un peu les fanatiques; ce seroit de lui faire faire dans l'église catholique de Berlin le service funèbre que nos prélats welches lui ont refusé." [27] The King readily acceeded to the demand and a Mass was duly celebrated on 30 May 1780. An account of the Mass appeared in several newspapers outside of France. The story, which was subsequently translated and sent to France, doubted that the French clergy had ever wished to deny a Catholic burial for

---

[23] *Ibid.*
[24] Quoted by Desnoiresterres, VIII, 433.
[25] Frédéric II, XV, 115.
[26] La Harpe, II, 346.
[27] Frédéric II, XV, 136-137.

Voltaire, because it was "chose que ce clergé si respectable n'eût pu faire sans violer les lois de la justice, sans blesser les principes de la bonne police, et sans donner à des haines particulières une influence incompatible avec la charité chrétienne, et avec toutes les vertus sincères et véritables." [28] With this lesson in Christian charity addressed to the French Church, d'Alembert could at last feel that the memory of Voltaire had been sufficiently vindicated.

The Academy, in the meantime, was still paying tribute to Voltaire. In 1779, after the inauguration of Ducis, there had been the St. Louis Day assembly when the prize for the best *Eloge de Voltaire* was awarded. The results of the contest were unusual that year. The entry which was judged superior to all others was anonymous. The Academy was then informed that the author wanted the Company to award the prize to the second place winner (Registres, III, 457). As a result, two *Eloges* were read at the public assembly of 25 August. The mystery was soon resolved: the anonymous writer was La Harpe, who, being a member of the Academy, was unable to take part in the contests. His wish to pay homage to his master had won over any other considerations. A few months later, in the Academy's meeting of 20 January 1780, La Harpe again honored the memory of the departed philosophe by reading excerpts from an *Eloge de Voltaire* he had written in prose (Registres, III, 465). A eulogy of Voltaire was once more the subject at a St. Louis Day assembly in 1782, when the winning entry of the poetry contest was a piece entitled "Voltaire et le Serf du mont Jura." That year, the Academy had left the contestants free to choose their own topics, and it seems that the winner owed his good fortune to the choice rather than to the treatment of his subject. Meister observed that the prize had been awarded principally because the winning poem gave "une nouvelle occasion de parler de M. de Voltaire, occasion qui ne saurait se renouveler assez souvent, ces messieurs sentant, et devant bien sentir tous les jours plus vivement l'extrême besoin de se couvrir de la gloire du grand homme qui n'est plus." [29]

Following this date, the celebration of Voltaire does not appear on the Academy's agenda for the remainder of the century. But then, for the time being, the topic had been exhausted. No other Acade-

---

[28] Quoted by Desnoiresterres, VIII, 444.
[29] Grimm, XIII, 197.

mician had ever been commemorated with such display nor with such insistence. For d'Alembert, who had made it a matter of policy to praise Voltaire, the celebrations he had organized represented a crowning achievement for his Academic career. He had been successful in paying a brilliant tribute to the patriarch of Ferney, as a friend, as a man of letters, as a philosophe. Yet, his own passing was noted principally for the lack of tributes. In 1784, shortly after his death, the Academy received an anonymous contribution destined to provide the award for an *Eloge de d'Alembert*. Two years later, not a single poem had been submitted, and the contest had to be prolonged by another year. There was no lack of entries for the other contests that year; sixty-eight works had been submitted for an *Eloge du prince de Brunswick,* forty for the "prix ordinaire," and twenty eight for the *Eloge de Louis XII.* [30] The "prix pour le meilleur catéchisme de morale" had also failed to attract entries, but it was no consolation for Condorcet, who had proposed the *Eloge de d'Alembert,* and who observed that "la plupart de ceux qui travaillent ordinairement pour ces prix avoient des obligations de plus d'un genre à Mr d'Alembert, et leur silence les expose au reproche d'ingratitude, à moins qu'ils ne permettent de le regarder comme un aveu de leur ignorance." [31]

The reproach was well founded. The French Academy in the second half of the eighteenth century owed a great part of its prestige to the efforts of d'Alembert, who had devoted himself to the Institution, yet his passing failed to draw much more than the usual recognition that accompanied departed members of the Company. Voltaire, on the other hand, was honored for his achievements as a philosophe and a man of letters. In effect, the Academy was simply repaying Voltaire for the brilliance his name had given to the entire Institution.

---

[30] *Ibid.,* XIV, 443.
[31] Frédéric II, XV, 280.

CONCLUSION

In the eyes of posterity Voltaire's renown would have been unaffected had he not been a member of the French Academy. On the other hand, it is certain that the prestige of the Institution would have suffered considerably if Voltaire's name had never appeared on its membership roster. In 1760, Pompignan had boasted that he would get Voltaire expelled from the Academy. A contemporary then remarked: "Si l'on rayoit M. de Voltaire du nombre des quarante, ce seroit ôter le chiffre, et... il ne resteroit que le zéro." [1] If we wish to determine Voltaire's contribution to the French Academy, we can first state that every literary production adding to the renown of the author enhanced the prestige of the Institution as well. In a more specific way, Voltaire's activities were of consequence on two occasions: he helped the Academy in 1760 by discrediting Pompignan and he played a determining role in the elections of 1771 by opposing de Brosses. Otherwise, he gave very little to the Academy, for his influence, until 1778, always remained minimal, and even then it failed to bring concrete results.

Yet, Voltaire had spent considerable time and effort in trying to inspire his fellow Academicians. He had exhorted them and had set the example, by words and by deeds. He was undoubtedly proud to be a member of the French Academy and was serious about his Academic responsibilities. His correspondence is revealing in this respect, and an exclamation such as "je suis saisi d'une indignation académique, quand je lis nos nouveaux livres" (Best. 8797, to d'Olivet, 22 January 1761), gives us a valuable glimpse of his thoughts. Voltaire's conception of the Academician's role stemmed from his inter-

---

[1] Favart, I, 46.

pretation of the Academy's role and importance. The principal concern of the Institution thus had to be the domain of French language and letters: it had been founded to preserve the purity of the language and to maintain the highest standards of taste in French letters. Voltaire's definition was faithful to the objectives set forth in the Company's statutes of 1635, and his criteria of purity and taste remained fundamentally the same as those applied in the previous century. Consequently, the foundation of the Academy represented a significant moment in the cultural history of his country: "Nous autres barbares qui existons d'hier,... nous n'avons été que des polissons en tout genre, jusqu'à l'établissement de l'académie, et au phénomène du Cid" (Best. 9165, to Mairan, 16 August 1761). He held to these views throughout his life, from the moment he first became seriously interested in the Company of Immortals. A few months before his death, he addressed the Academy in the preface to *Irène*: "Si votre compagnie fut nécessaire à la France par son institution, dans un temps où nous n'avions aucun ouvrage de génie écrit d'un style pur et noble, elle est plus nécessaire que jamais dans la multitude des productions que fait naître aujourd'hui le goût généralement répandu de la littérature" (Moland, VII, 325).

This attitude had evolved somewhat during the philosophic offensive of the sixties, when Voltaire seconded d'Alembert's efforts, but the patriarch's interest in the cause of the "brothers" was never in conflict with his concern for literature. Furthermore, when around 1770 increasing pressure from the government forced the philosophes to moderate their stance in the Academy, Voltaire realized that the Institution could not become the citadel of philosophes contemplated by d'Alembert. In this respect, he had no illusions about the French Academy. It remained under the tutelage of the King and the philosophy it espoused was a moderate and mundane variety that could not afford to offend the more conservative, clerical faction of the membership. The members of the clergy still made up a considerable percentage and provided a source of humor for Voltaire, who pointed out to d'Alembert that he was the "secrétaire du clergé sous le nom de secrétaire de l'académie" (Best. 18777, 8 February 1776). In a similar vein, Condorcet told Voltaire the anecdote of the bishop who had complained to his fellow clergymen by saying: "Qui le croirait, m.m.? le sanctuaire des lettres est devenu le repaire de l'incrédulité et de l'irréligion." The statement had met with an instant rebuttal: "Mais m., ... vous n'y songez pas! Nous sommes 7 évêques dans l'Académie" (Best. 18480, 12 August 1775). Most of the ecclesiastical members of the Academy, however, were no longer the resolute opponents of the philosophes they had once been. So long as they were not forced to go against the policies of the French Church, they could very well be on the best of terms with members of the philosophe clan. D'Alembert's commentary on the election of Loménie de Brienne, the Archbishop of Toulouse, shows that this tolerance was mutual: "Nous avons en lui un très bon confrère, qui sera certainement utile aux lettres, et à la philosophie, pourvû que la philosophie ne lui lie pas les mains par un excès de licence, ou que le cri général ne l'oblige d'agir contre son gré" (Best. 15832, to Voltaire, December 1770). Voltaire was very understanding in this respect and was interested in maintaining friendly relations with every member of the Academy. His tolerance of Academicians who held to philosophies that were considerably different from his indicates simply that he accepted the Academy for what it was: a brilliant symbol of the leading position that French arts and letters held in Europe.

On the other hand, Voltaire never abandoned his illusions about the practical role of the Academy. It is probable that had he lived longer, he would have seen that the Institution, as it had evolved in the second part of the eighteenth century, was unable to carry out serious linguistic projects. The importance it accorded its public functions, the time it spent on its contests in poetry and eloquence had given it an increasingly ceremonial role. In an age when the art of public speaking was highly esteemed, the Academy catered to an ever-growing audience which was primarily interested in its discourses. After they were printed, these discourses remained equally popular, as d'Alembert once explained to Voltaire: "Vous croyez donc qu'on ne vend que cent exemplaires d'un discours de l'académie? Détrompez vous; ces sortes d'ouvrages sont plus achetés que vous ne pensez; tous les prédicateurs, avocats, et autres gens de la ville et de la province, qui font métier de paroles, se jettent à corps perdu sur cette marchandise" (Best. 12988, 26 January 1767). Voltaire never understood the real nature of the Academy because he remained absent from it for the greater part of his Academic career. Perhaps it was fortunate that he did not have the occasion to participate fully in the Company's activities. At the time of his election, a contemporary observer made a perceptive assessment of the new Academician by commenting the inaugural discourse: "J'y admire le profond littérateur,... j'y trouve et j'admire *l'historien de l'esprit humain*; mais je ne saurais y reconnaître le récipiendaire académicien, l'homme qui court une carrière, où se sont signalés tant de brillants génies" (Best. 3102, La Montaigne to Acary, 12 June 1746). Voltaire's absence and later his death saved the relationship from a conflict which would have been inevitable in a close and prolonged contact, considering the respective natures of the member and of the organization.

As it was, the relationship was characterized by feelings of respect on both sides and continued improving until the day of Voltaire's death. After the patriarch had passed away, the Academy became a veritable family to him, jealously guarding his memory. The accusation of "adultère spirituel" which the Academy directed at Mme Denis after her marriage in 1779 was a clear expression of this possessiveness. There had been a time when the Academy had shown great reluctance in accepting Voltaire as its member. A half-century later, when the Revolution came, it was proud to display the ties that linked it to the great philosophe. For many, the Company had veritably become the embodiment of the literary spirit of Voltaire. Thus in 1791, when the remains of Voltaire were brought back to Paris in a grandiose celebration, the *Registres* recorded: "Le Directoire, considérant l'Académie françoise comme la famille littéraire de Mr de Voltaire, il avait été arrêté qu'elle aurait sa place dans cette cérémonie, autour du cercueil, conjointement avec la famille de Mr de Voltaire" (Registres, III, 644). The Academy could never have become Voltaire's "famille littéraire" before his death; it would have been unable to meet his requirements. And yet, in spite of all the differences and misunderstandings, Voltaire was a part of the Academy, just as they both were a part of their age, bringing it the literary elegance that the Ancien Régime held in such high esteem. A revolutionary decree abolished the Academy in 1793. It was inevitable that, since the Age of Voltaire had ended, the Company had to close its doors. [2]

---

[2] The Company was reestablished, in a dismembered form, when the *Institut national* was created in 1795. The French Academy finally recovered its name and former statutes in 1816, by virtue of a royal ordonnance.

APPENDIX A

Members of the French Academy in 1731, in the order of their chairs:

1. cardinal de Fleury
2. abbé Bignon
3. abbé de Rothelin
4. Crébillon
5. Roland-Malet
6. abbé Mongault
7. Languet de Gergy, évêque de Sens
8. maréchal d'Estrées
9. Bussy-Rabutin, évêque de Luçon
10. abbé de Saint-Pierre [1]
11. Portail
12. président Bouhier
13. abbé Sallier
14. duc de Richelieu
15. Gondrin d'Antin, évêque de Langres
16. maréchal de Villars
17. Coislin, évêque de Metz
18. de Boze
19. président Hénault
20. abbé Gédoyn
21. Fleuriau de Marville
22. Fontenelle

---

[1] Chair No. 10 was left vacant after the exclusion of the abbé de Saint-Pierre in 1718 and remained unoccupied until his death in 1743.

23. cardinal de Rohan
24. abbé Alary
25. abbé d'Olivet
26. Destouches
27. marquis de Sainte-Aulaire
28. abbé Dubos
29. Danchet
30. abbé d'Houtteville
31. Hardion
32. Adam
33. cardinal de Polignac
34. Amelot
35. Mongin, évêque de Bazas
36. duc de Saint-Aignan
37. Mirabaud
38. Montesquieu
39. Massillon, évêque de Clermont
40. Caumartin, évêque de Blois

APPENDIX B

Members of the French Academy in 1746, following the election of Voltaire (an asterisk indicates that the occupancy has changed since 1731):

* 1. Luynes, évêque de Bayeux
* 2. Bignon (Armand Jérôme)
* 3. abbé Girard
  4. Crébillon
* 5. Boyer, évêque de Mirepoix
  6. abbé Mongault
  7. Languet de Gergy, évêque de Sens
* 8. cardinal de Rohan Soubise
* 9. Foncemagne
*10. Maupertuis
*11. La Chaussée
*12. Voltaire
  13. abbé Sallier
  14. duc de Richelieu
*15. Dupré de Saint-Maur
*16. duc de Villars
*17. Surian, évêque de Vence
  18. de Boze
  19. président Hénault
*20. abbé de Bernis
*21. abbé Terrasson
  22. Fontenelle
  23. cardinal de Rohan
  24. abbé Alary

25. abbé d'Olivet
26. Destouches
*27. Mairan
*28. abbé du Resnel
29. Danchet
*30. Marivaux
31. Hardion
*32. abbé Séguy
*33. abbé de Saint-Cyr
34. Amelot
35. Mongin, évêque de Bazas
36. duc de Saint-Aignan
37. Mirabaud
38. Montesquieu
*39. duc de Nivernais
*40. Moncrif

APPENDIX C

Members of the French Academy in 1761, at the time of Pompignan's reception (a hyphen indicates a change since 1746):

1. cardinal de Luynes
2. Bignon (Armand-Jérôme)
-3. marquis de Paulmy
4. Crébillon
-5. abbé Boismont
-6. Duclos
-7. Buffon
-8. Montazet, archevêque de Lyon
9. Foncemagne
-10. Pompignan
-11. Bougainville
12. Voltaire
13. abbé Sallier
14. duc de Richelieu
15. Dupré de Saint-Maur
16. duc de Villars
-17. d'Alembert
-18. comte de Clermont
19. président Hénault
20. cardinal de Bernis
-21. comte de Bissy
-22. Séguier
-23. Vauréal, évêque de Rennes
24. abbé Alary
25. abbé d'Olivet

-26. Sainte-Palaye
27. Mairan
28. abbé du Resnel
-29. Gresset
30. Marivaux
31. Hardion
32. abbé Séguy
33. abbé de Saint-Cyr
-34. maréchal de Belle-Isle
-35. abbé de La Ville
36. duc de Saint-Aignan
37. Mirabaud
-38. Châteaubrun
39. duc de Nivernois
40. Moncrif

BIBLIOGRAPHY

LIST OF WORKS CONSULTED

Albert-Buisson, François. *Les Quarante au temps des lumières*. Paris: A. Fayard, 1960.

Alembert, Jean Lerond d'. *Œuvres de d'Alembert*. Vols. II and III. 1921; rpt. Geneva: Slatkine, 1967.

L'Année littéraire, ou suite des lettres sur quelques écrits de ce temps, par m. Fréron. Vol. VII. 1760; rpt. Geneva: Slatkine, 1966.

Argenson, René-Louis de Voyer, marquis d'. *Journal et Mémoires du Marquis d'Argenson*. Ed. J. B. Rathery. 9 vols. Paris: Vve Jules Renouard, 1859-1867.

Arnold, Matthew. *Essays in Criticism*. First series. London: Macmillan and Co., 1910.

Aubertin, Charles. *L'Esprit public au XVIIIe siècle*. Paris: Perrin et Cie., 1889.

Bachaumont, Louis Petit de. *Mémoires secrets pour servir à l'histoire de la république des lettres en France*. 36 vols. London: John Adamson, 1777-1789.

Bachman, Albert. *Censorship in France from 1715 to 1750*. New York: Institute of French Studies, Columbia Univ., 1934.

Barbier, Edmond Jean François. *Chronique de la régence et du règne de Louis XV (1718-1763), ou Journal de Barbier*. 8 vols. Paris: Charpentier, 1885.

Barr, Mary-Margaret H. *A Bibliography of Writings on Voltaire, (1825-1925)*. New York: Institute of French Studies, 1929.

——— and Frederick A. Spear. *Quarante années d'études voltairiennes*. Paris: Armand Colin, 1968.

Belin, J. P. *Le Mouvement philosophique de 1748 à 1789*. Paris: Belin Frères, 1913.

Bellessort, André. *Essai sur Voltaire*. Paris: Perrin et Cie., 1950.

Bernis, François Joachim de Pierre, Cardinal de. *Mémoires et lettres*. Ed. Frédéric Masson. 2 vols. Paris: Plon et Cie., 1878.

Besterman, Theodore. *Voltaire*. New York: Harcourt, Brace and World, 1969.

———. *Voltaire on Shakespeare*. Studies on Voltaire and the Eighteenth Century, Vol. LIV. Geneva: Institut et Musée Voltaire, 1967.

Binaut, L. A. "Voltaire à l'Académie." *Le Correspondant*, VII (1844), 681-697.

Boissier, Gaston. *L'Académie française sous l'Ancien Régime.* Paris: Hachette, 1909.

Boutry, Maurice. "Le Cardinal de Tencin et le Saint-Siège. Lettres inédites du Pape Benoît XIV." *Revue des Etudes historiques,* 65e année (1899), 427-436.

―――. *Une créature du cardinal Dubois: intrigues et missions diplomatiques du cardinal de Tencin.* Paris: H. Vivien, 1902.

Brandes, Georg. *Voltaire.* Trans. Otto Kruger and Pierce Butler. 2 vols. New York: Tudor Publishing Co., 1930.

Broglie, Emmanuel de. *Les Portefeuilles du président Bouhier.* Paris: Hachette, 1896.

Brunel, Lucien. *Les Philosophes et l'Académie française au dix-huitième siècle.* Paris: Hachette, 1884.

Buffon. *Correspondance inédite de Buffon.* 2 vols. Paris: Hachette, 1860.

Cabeen, David C., ed. *A Critical Bibliography of French Literature.* Vol. IV: *The Eighteenth Century.* Syracuse, N. Y.: Syracuse Univ. Press, 1951.

―――. *A Critical Bibliography of French Literature.* Vol. IV A: *The Eighteenth Century: Supplement.* Ed. by R. A. Brooks. Syracuse, N. Y.: Syracuse Univ. Press, 1968.

Cardahi, Choucri. *Regards sous la Coupole: histoire et petite histoire de l'Académie française.* Paris: Mame, 1967.

Cassirer, Ernst. *The Philosophy of the Enlightenment.* Tr. James P. Pettegrove and Fritz C. A. Koelln. Princeton: Princeton Univ. Press, 1951.

Caussy, Fernand. "Voltaire au Pays de Gex." *Mercure de France,* vol. 95 (Janvier-Février 1912), 724-744.

Choix de discours de réception à l'Académie française. 2 vols. Paris: Demonville, 1808.

Cioranescu, Alexandre. *Bibliographie de la littérature française du dix-huitième siècle.* 3 vols. Paris: Centre national de la recherche scientifique, 1969.

Collé, Charles. *Journal et Mémoires sur les hommes de lettres du règne de Louis XV.* 3 vols. Paris: Firmin Didot, 1868.

Conlon, P. M. *Voltaire's Literary Career from 1728 to 1750.* Studies on Voltaire and the Eighteenth Century, Vol. XIV. Geneva: Institut et Musée Voltaire, 1961.

Correspondance du cardinal de Tencin, ministre d'Etat, et de Mme de Tencin, sa sœur, avec le duc de Richelieu sur les intrigues de la cour de France depuis 1742 jusqu'en 1757. Paris: 1790.

Crouslé, Léon. *La Vie et les œuvres de Voltaire.* Paris: Champion, 1899.

Cunisset-Carnot. "La Querelle du président de Brosses avec Voltaire." *La Revue des Deux Mondes,* 15 February 1888, pp. 879-895.

Desnoiresterres, Gustave. *Voltaire et la société au dix-huitième siècle.* 8 vols. Paris: Didier et Cie., 1871.

Diderot. *Correspondance.* Ed. Georges Roth. Vols. III and IV. Paris: Editions de Minuit, 1955-1966.

Duclos, Charles. *Correspondance de Charles Duclos.* Ed. Jacques Brengues. Saint-Brieuc: Presses Universitaires de Bretagne, 1970.

―――. *Œuvres complètes.* Vol. I. Paris: A. Belin, 1821.

Du Deffand, Marie Chamrond, marquise. *Correspondance complète.* Ed. Lescure. 2 vols. Paris: Plon, 1865.

Faur, Louis-François. *Vie privée du Maréchal de Richelieu.* 3 vols. Paris: Buisson, 1791.

Favart, Charles S. *Mémoires et Correspondance littéraires, dramatiques et anecdotiques.* 2 vols. Paris: L. Collin, 1808.
Fellows, Otis E. *From Voltaire to "La Nouvelle Critique": Problems and Personalities.* Geneva: Droz, 1970.
Fields, Madelaine. "Voltaire et le Mercure de France." *Studies on Voltaire and the Eighteenth Century,* XX, 175-216. Geneva: Institut et Musée Voltaire, 1962.
François, Alexis. *La Grammaire du Purisme et l'Académie française au XVIIIe siècle.* Paris: G. Bellais, 1905.
Frédéric II. *Œuvres posthumes.* Vol. XV. Berlin: Voss and Decker, 1788.
Galiani, abbé F. *Correspondance avec Mme d'Epinay, Mme Necker, Mme Geoffrin Etc., Diderot, Grimm, D'Alembert, De Sartine, D'Holbach Etc.* 2 vols. Paris: Calmann Lévy, 1890.
Gassier, Emile. *Les Cinq cents Immortels: histoire de l'Académie française, 1634-1906.* Paris: Henri Jouve, 1906.
Gaxotte, Pierre. "Autour de Voltaire." *La Revue des Deux mondes,* 15 February 1951, pp. 713-722.
Gay, Peter. *The Party of Humanity: Essays in the French Enlightenment.* New York: Alfred A. Knopf, 1964.
———. *Voltaire's Politics: The Poet as Realist.* Princeton: Princeton Univ. Press, 1959.
Grimm, baron Friedrich Melchior von. *Correspondance littéraire, philosophique et critique par Grimm, Diderot, Raynal, Meister, Etc.* 16 vols. Paris: Garnier Frères, 1877-1882.
Grimsley, Ronald. *Jean d'Alembert.* Oxford: Clarendon Press, 1963.
Havinga, Jan Christiaan Adolph. *Les Nouvelles ecclésiastiques dans leur lutte contre l'esprit philosophique.* Amersfoort: S. W. Melchior, 1925.
Heeckeren, Emile de. "Benoît XIV et le cardinal de Tencin." *Bulletin historique du Diocèse de Lyon,* Vol. VIII, No. 63 (1910), 65-80.
Henriot, Emile. *Courrier littéraire: XVIIIe siècle.* Paris: Editions Marcel Daubin, 1945.
Houssaye, Arsène. *Histoire du 41ème fauteuil de l'Académie française.* Paris: Lecour, 1855.
Jacquart, Jean. *L'abbé Trublet critique et moraliste.* Paris: Auguste Picard, 1926.
Journal encyclopédique ou universel, par une société des gens de lettres. Vol. XVII. Janvier-Juin 1764; rpt. Geneva: Slatkine, 1967.
La Harpe, Jean-François. *Correspondance littéraire.* 6 vols. Paris: Migneret, 1804-1807.
Lanfrey, Pierre. *L'Eglise et les philosophes au XVIIIe siècle.* Paris: V. Lecou, 1855.
———. *Histoire politique des papes.* Paris: Charpentier, 1880.
Lanson, Gustave. *Manuel bibliographique de la littérature française moderne: XVIIIe siècle.* Vol. III. Paris: Hachette, 1921.
———. *Voltaire.* Paris: Hachette, 1906.
Léouzon, Le Duc, L. *Voltaire et la police.* Paris: Ambroise Bray, 1867.
Longchamp, Sébastien G., and Jean Louis Wagnière. *Mémoires sur Voltaire, et sur ses ouvrages par Longchamp et Wagnière.* 2 vols. Paris: Aimé André, 1826.
Lowenstein, Robert. *Voltaire as an Historian of Seventeenth Century French Drama.* Baltimore: The Johns Hopkins Press, 1935.

Luynes, Albert, duc de. *Mémoires du duc de Luynes sur la cour de Louis XV (1735-1758)*. 17 vols. Paris: Firmin Didot, 1860-1865.
Marais, Mathieu. *Journal et Mémoires sur la Régence et le Règne de Louis XV*. Ed. Lescure. 4 vols. Paris: Firmin Didot, 1863-1868.
Marmontel, Jean-François. *Œuvres complètes*. Vol. I. Paris: Verdière, 1818-1819.
Martini, Mario Maria. "Il Presidente de Brosses e Voltaire." *Le Opere e i Giorni*, XVI (January 1937), 24-28.
Marville, Claude Henri Feydeau de. *Lettres au ministre Maurepas*. Ed. A. de Boislisle. Paris: Champion, 1896.
Masson, Frédérick. *L'Académie française: 1629-1793*. Paris: Paul Ollendorf, 1912.
Mathiez, Albert. "Les Philosophes et le pouvoir au milieu du XVIIIe siècle." *Annales historiques de la Révolution française*, XII (1935), 1-12.
Mémoires pour l'histoire des sciences et des beaux-arts. 1746.
Mercure de France. 1746.
Mesnard, Paul. *Histoire de l'Académie française depuis sa fondation jusqu'en 1830*. Paris: Charpentier, 1857.
Micard, Etienne. *Un écrivain académique au XVIIIe siècle: Antoine Léonard Thomas*. Paris: Champion, 1924.
Montesquieu, Charles-Louis de Secondat de. *Œuvres complètes*. Paris: Gallimard, 1949.
Morelli, Emilia, ed. *La Lettere di Benedetto XIV al Card. de Tencin*. Rome: Edizioni di Storia e Letteratura, 1955.
Mornet, Daniel. *Les Origines intellectuelles de la Révolution française*. Paris: A. Colin, 1933.
Naves, Raymond. *Le Goût de Voltaire*. Paris: Garnier Frères, 1938.
——. *Voltaire et l'Encyclopédie*. Paris: Les Editions des Presses modernes, 1938.
Nisard, Charles. *Les Ennemis de Voltaire*. Paris: Amyot, 1853.
Nivat, Jean. "Voltaire et les ministres." *La Table Ronde*, No. 122 (1958), pp. 44-57.
Les Nouvelles ecclésiastiques, ou Mémoires pour servir à l'histoire de la Constitution Unigenitus, pour le années 1728-1782. 1746 and 1750.
Olivet, Pierre-Joseph Thoulier d'. *Remarques sur la langue françoise*. Paris: Barbou, 1767.
Ormesson, Wladimir. *Le Clergé et l'Académie*. Paris: Wesmael-Charlier, 1965.
Pappas, John N. *The Journal de Trévoux and the Philosophes*. Studies on Voltaire and the Eighteenth Century, Vol. III. Geneva: Institut et Musée Voltaire, 1957.
——. *Voltaire and d'Alembert*. Bloomington: Indiana Univ. Press, 1962.
——. "Voltaire et la guerre civile philosophique." *Revue d'histoire littéraire de la France*, 61e année, No. 4 (1961), 525-549.
Pastor, Ludwig. *The History of the Popes from the Close of the Middle Ages*. Trans. F. I. Antrobus and E. F. Peeler. Vol. XXXVI. London: K. Paul, Trench, Trubner, 1938-1968.
Pellisson-Fontanier, P. and Pierre-Joseph Thoulier d'Olivet. *Histoire de l'Académie française par Pellisson et d'Olivet*. 2 vols. Paris: Didier et Cie., 1858.
Pellisson, Maurice. *Les Hommes de lettres au XVIIIe siècle*. Paris: Armand Colin, 1911.

Peter, René. *Vie secrète de l'Académie française.* 4 vols. Paris: Librairie des Champs-Elysées, 1934.

Picot, M. *Mémoires pour servir à l'histoire ecclésiastique pendant le dix-huitième siècle.* 7 vols. Paris: Adrien Le Clère, 1853.

Pomeau, René. *La Religion de Voltaire.* Paris: Nizet, 1956.

Ranke, Leopold von. *The History of the Popes during the Last Four Centuries.* Trans. E. Foster. Vol. III. London: Bell and sons, 1908.

Ravaisson, François. *Archives de la Bastille.* Vol. XII. Paris: Durand, 1866-1904.

Recueil des pièces d'éloquence et de poésie qui ont remporté les Prix de l'Académie Françoise, depuis 1747 jusqu'en 1753. Avec les discours et pièces de poésie prononcez ou lus dans l'Académie. Paris: Bernard Brunet, 1753.

Les Registres de l'Académie française. Ed. Camille Doucet. 4 vols. Paris: Firmin Didot, 1895-1906.

Rezler, Marta. "The Voltaire-d'Alembert Correspondence: an Historical and Bibliographical Re-appraisal." *Studies on Voltaire and the Eighteenth Century,* XX, 9-140. Geneva: Institut et Musée Voltaire, 1962.

Robertson, D. Maclaren. *A History of the French Academy (1635-1910).* New York: G. W. Dillingham Co., 1910.

Roustan, Mario. *Les Philosophes et la société française au XVIIIe siècle.* Lyon: A. Rey, 1906.

Rouxel, Albert. *Chronique des élections à l'Académie française.* Paris: Firmin Didot, 1888.

Sainte-Beuve. "Voltaire et le président de Brosses, ou une intrigue académique au XVIIIe siècle." *Causeries du Lundi,* VII, 105-126. Paris: Garnier Frères, 1852.

Sareil, Jean. "Quelques lettres de Voltaire et de ses amis." *Revue d'histoire littéraire de la France,* IV (July-August 1970), 657-658.

———. *Les Tencin.* Geneva: Droz, 1969.

———. "Voltaire et le cardinal de Fleury." *Revue annuelle de la Société française d'étude du XVIIIe siècle,* II, 39-76. Paris: Garnier Frères, 1970.

Segrais, Jean Renaud de. *Œuvres diverses.* 2 vols. Amsterdam: François Changuion, 1723.

Tastet, Tyrtée. *Histoire des quarante fauteuils de l'Académie française depuis la fondation jusqu'à nos jours.* Paris: Lacroix-Camon, 1855.

Torrey, Norman L. *The Spirit of Voltaire.* New York: Columbia Univ. Press, 1938.

———. "Voltaire's Reaction to Diderot." *PMLA,* L (1935), 1107-1143.

Trublet, abbé Nicolas. *La Correspondance de l'abbé Trublet.* Ed. J. Jacquet. Paris: Auguste Picard, 1926.

Unger, Otto. *Voltaire's Beurteilung Corneille's und seine eigenen dramatischen Theorien und Neuerungen.* Crimmitschau: Robert Kaab, 1899.

Vercruysse, J. "Bibliographie des écrits français relatifs à Voltaire, 1719-1830." *Studies on Voltaire and the Eighteenth Century,* LX, 7-71. Geneva: Institut et Musée Voltaire, 1968.

Vernier, Léon. *Etude sur Voltaire grammairien et la grammaire au XVIIIe siècle.* Paris: Hachette, 1888.

Voltaire, François Marie Arouet. *Lettres philosophiques.* Ed. Gustave Lanson. 2 vols. Paris: Hachette, 1915-1917.

Voltaire, François Marie Arouet. *Lettres philosophiques.* Ed. Raymond Naves. Paris: Garnier Frères, 1964.
———. *Œuvres complètes.* Ed. Louis Moland. 52 vols. Paris: Garnier Frères, 1877-1885.
———. *Voltaire's Correspondence.* Ed. Theodore Besterman. 107 vols. Geneva: Institut et Musée Voltaire, 1953-1965.
"Voltaire and the Président de Brosses." *The New Monthly Magazine,* CXIV (1858), 367-378.
Voltariana ou éloges amphigouriques de Fr. Marie Arrouet. Paris: 1748.
Wade, Ira O. "The Epître à Uranie." *PMLA,* XLVII (1932), 1066-1112.
———. *The Intellectual Development of Voltaire.* Princeton: Princeton Univ. Press, 1969.
———. *Voltaire and Madame du Châtelet.* Princeton: Princeton Univ. Press, 1941.
Waldinger, Renée. *Voltaire and Reform in the Light of the French Revolution.* Geneva: Droz, 1959.
Williams, David. *Voltaire: Literary Critic.* Studies on Voltaire and the Eighteenth Century, Vol. XLVIII. Geneva: Institut et Musée Voltaire, 1966.
Wilson, Arthur M. *Diderot.* New York: Oxford Univ. Press, 1972.

NORTH CAROLINA STUDIES IN THE ROMANCE LANGUAGES AND LITERATURES

I.S.B.N. Prefix 0-88438

Recent Titles

THE OLD PORTUGUESE "VIDA DE SAM BERNARDO," EDITED FROM ALCOBAÇA MANUSCRIPT ccxci/200, WITH INTRODUCTION, LINGUISTIC STUDY, NOTES, TABLE OF PROPER NAMES, AND GLOSSARY, by Lawrence A. Sharpe. 1971. (No. 103). -903-0.

A CRITICAL AND ANNOTATED EDITION OF LOPE DE VEGA'S "LAS ALMENAS DE TORO," by Thomas E. Case. 1971. (No. 104). -904-9.

LOPE DE VEGA'S "LO QUE PASA EN UNA TARDE," A CRITICAL, ANNOTATED EDITION OF THE AUTOGRAPH MANUSCRIPT, by Richard Angelo Picerno. 1971. (No. 105). -905-7.

OBJECTIVE METHODS FOR TESTING AUTHENTICITY AND THE STUDY OF TEN DOUBTFUL "COMEDIAS" ATTRIBUTED TO LOPE DE VEGA, by Fred M. Clark. 1971. (No. 106). -906-5.

THE ITALIAN VERB. A MORPHOLOGICAL STUDY, by Frede Jensen. 1971. (No. 107). -907-3.

A CRITICAL EDITION OF THE OLD PROVENÇAL EPIC "DAUREL ET BETON," WITH NOTES AND PROLEGOMENA, by Arthur S. Kimmel. 1971. (No. 108). -908-1.

FRANCISCO RODRIGUES LOBO: DIALOGUE AND COURTLY LORE IN RENAISSANCE PORTUGAL, by Richard A. Preto-Rodas, 1971. (No. 109). -909-X.

RAIMON VIDAL: POETRY AND PROSE, edited by W. H. W. Field. 1971. (No. 110). -910-3.

RELIGIOUS ELEMENTS IN THE SECULAR LYRICS OF THE TROUBADOURS, by Raymond Gay-Crosier. 1971. (No. 111). -911-1.

THE SIGNIFICANCE OF DIDEROT'S "ESSAI SUR LE MERITE ET LA VERTU," by Gordon B. Walters. 1971. (No. 112). -912-X.

PROPER NAMES IN THE LYRICS OF THE TROUBADOURS, by Frank M. Chambers. 1971. (No. 113). -913-8.

STUDIES IN HONOR OF MARIO A. PEI, edited by John Fisher and Paul A. Gaeng. 1971. (No. 114). -914-6.

DON MANUEL CAÑETE, CRONISTA LITERARIO DEL ROMANTICISMO Y DEL POSROMANTICISMO EN ESPAÑA, por Donald Allen Randolph. 1972. (No. 115). -915-4.

THE TEACHINGS OF SAINT LOUIS. A CRITICAL TEXT, by David O'Connell. 1972. (No. 116). -916-2.

HIGHER, HIDDEN ORDER: DESIGN AND MEANING IN THE ODES OF MALHERBE, by David Lee Rubin. 1972. (No. 117). -917-0.

JEAN DE LE MOTE "LE PARFAIT DU PAON," édition critique par Richard J. Carey. 1972. (No. 118). -918-9.

CAMUS' HELLENIC SOURCES, by Paul Archambault. 1972. (No. 119). -919-7.

FROM VULGAR LATIN TO OLD PROVENÇAL, by Frede Jensen. 1972 (No. 120). -920-0.

GOLDEN AGE DRAMA IN SPAIN: GENERAL CONSIDERATION AND UNUSUAL FEATURES, by Sturgis E. Leavitt. 1972. (No. 121). -921-9.

THE LEGEND OF THE "SIETE INFANTES DE LARA" (*Refundición toledana de la crónica de 1344* versión), study and edition by Thomas A. Lathrop. 1972. (No. 122). -922-7.

STRUCTURE AND IDEOLOGY IN BOIARDO'S "ORLANDO INNAMORATO", by Andrea di Tommaso. 1972. (No. 123). -923-5.

STUDIES IN HONOR OF ALFRED G. ENGSTROM, edited by Robert T. Cargo and Emanuel J. Mickel, Jr. 1972. (No. 124). -924-3.

NORTH CAROLINA STUDIES IN THE ROMANCE LANGUAGES AND LITERATURES

I.S.B.N. Prefix 0-88438

Recent Titles

A CRITICAL EDITION WITH INTRODUCTION AND NOTES OF GIL VICENTE'S "FLORESTA DE ENGAÑOS", by Constantine Christopher Stathatos. 1972. (No. 125). *-925-1.*

LI ROMANS DE WITASSE LE MOINE. *Roman du treizième siècle.* Édité d'après le manuscrit, fonds français 1553, de la Bibliothèque Nationale, Paris, par Denis Joseph Conlon. 1972. (No. 126). *-926-X.*

EL CRONISTA PEDRO DE ESCAVIAS. UNA VIDA DEL SIGLO XV, by Juan Bautista Avalle-Arce. 1972. (No. 127). *-927-8.*

AN EDITION OF THE FIRST ITALIAN TRANSLATION OF THE CELESTINA, by Kathleen Kish. 1973. (No. 128). *-928-6.*

MOLIERE MOCKED: THREE CONTEMPORARY HOSTILE COMEDIES, by Frederick W. Vogler. 1973. (No. 129). *-929-4.*

INDEX ANALYTIQUE DE "CHATEAUBRIAND ET SON GROUPE LITTERAIRE SOUS L'EMPIRE" DE SAINTE-BEUVE, by Lorin A. Uffenbeck. 1973. (No. 130). *-930-8.*

THE ORIGINS OF THE BAROQUE CONCEPT OF PEREGRINATIO, by Juergen S. Hahn. 1973. (No. 131). *-931-6.*

THE "AUTO SACRAMENTAL" AND THE PARABLE IN THE SIXTEENTH AND SEVENTEENTH CENTURIES, by Donald T. Dietz. 1973. (No. 132). *-932-4.*

FRANCISCO DE OSUNA AND THE SPIRIT OF THE LETTER, by Laura Calvert. 1973. (No. 133). *-933-2.*

ITINERARIO DI AMORE: DIALETTICA DI AMORE E MORTE NELLA VITA NUOVA, by Margherita de Bonfils Templer. 1973. (No. 134). *-934-0.*

L'IMAGINATION POETIQUE CHEZ DU BARTAS, ELEMENTS DE SENSIBILITE BAROQUE DANS LA "CREATION DU MONDE," by Bruno Braunrot. 1973. (No. 135). *-935-9.*

ARTUS DÉSIRÉ, PRIEST AND PAMPHLETEER OF THE SIXTEENTH CENTURY, by Frank Giese 1973. (No. 136). *-936-7.*

JARDIN DE NOBLES DONZELLAS BY FRAY MARTÍN DE CÓRDOBA, by Harriet Goldberg. 1974. (No. 137). *-937-5.*

MOLIERE: TRADITIONS IN CRITICISM, by Laurence Romero. 1974 (Essays, No. 1). *-001-7.*

STUDIES IN TIRSO, I, by Ruth Lee Kennedy. 1974. (Essays, No. 3). *-003-3.*

LAS MEMORIAS DE GONZALO FERNÁNDEZ DE OVIEDO, Vols. I and II, by Juan Bautista Avalle-Arce. 1974. (Texts, Textual Studies, and Translations, Nos. 1 and 2). *-401-2; 402-0.*

ESTUDIOS DE LITERATURA HISPANOAMERICANA EN HONOR A JOSÉ J. ARROM, edited by Andrew P. Debicki and Enrique Pupo-Walker. 1975. (Symposia, No. 2). *952-9.*

When ordering please cite the *ISBN Prefix* plus the last four digits for each title.

Send orders to:

    University of North Carolina Press
    Chapel Hill
    North Carolina 27514
    U. S. A.

The Department of Romance Studies Digital Arts and Collaboration Lab at the University of North Carolina at Chapel Hill is proud to support the digitization of the North Carolina Studies in the Romance Languages and Literatures series.

www.ingramcontent.com/pod-product-compliance
Lightning Source LLC
Chambersburg PA
CBHW020418230426
43663CB00007BA/1224